# ENDORSEMENTS

I am happy to endorse the powerful book *From The Craft To Christ* by S.A. Tower. This powerful message opens one's eyes to the reality and danger of demonic involvement through Wicca and the occult. This book does not simply expose the problem... it gives a clear path to freedom.

~ **Dr. Ron Phillips**,
Author of 21 books including the award winning *Everyone's Guide to Demons and Spiritual Warfare*

*From The Craft to Christ* offers the reader an intimate and inside look at the perspective of those bound by the sin of Wicca and witchcraft... then presenting the humbling challenge to reach out with the Father's Love as we should anyone caught in any bondage. A truly "eye opening" work!

~ **Dr. Robert Stearns**,
Executive Director of Eagles' Wings Ministries

*From The Craft to Christ* serves as a catalytic narrative of hope and redemption for those darkened by the occult. In a world full of moral relativism, cultural decadence, spiritual apathy and darkened by the powers of darkness, S.A. Tower shines the light of Christ on the stand of lives emancipated from bondage by the blood of the Lamb.

~ **Rev. Samuel Rodriguez**,
President - Hispanic Evangelical Association,
National Hispanic Christian Leadership Conference

*From The Craft to Christ* is a powerful demonstration of God's unceasing love to break into the Kingdom of Darkness and liberate those held captive by Satan's power. A must read!

~ **Robby Dawkins**,
International Vineyard Evangelist
Author of *"Do What Jesus Did"*
Featured in the films *"Furious Love"* and *"Father of Lights"*

As a woman of depth who has relied on my faith to endure life's trials and tribulations, I can attest how the power of prayer has impacted and blessed my life. In **From The Craft to Christ**, Author S. A. Tower shares the deeply moving stories of those who many would believe were beyond God's grace ... only to experience a divine intervention, redemption, and the results of prayer warriors working behind the scenes who never gave up hope.

~ **Suzanne Corso**,
N.Y. Times Best-Selling Author

In her second book about witchcraft, Ally Tower provides the Church with a power resource of practical, accurate information and action steps a local church or ministry can implement to set people free. I highly recommend this valuable book to every pastor and church leader as well as any person who needs to be delivered from darkness into the marvelous light of Jesus Christ.

~ **Dr. Larry Keefauver**,
Best-Selling Author and International Teacher

This is an excellent book, full of helpful insights that only could come from someone who has been there. The teaching is sound and it also gives great ways to reach out to wiccans and show the love of God to them.

~ **Dr. Carol Hansen-Robeson**,
Co-author of *Strongman's His Name,
What's His Game? I and II*

***From The Craft to Christ*** is a powerful book for several reasons. First, it is written with sympathetic kindness and genuine respect toward those who have sincerely sought for fulfillment in Wicca and witchcraft, instead of offering harsh condemnation. The latter only serves to build walls, not bridges. I call it "confrontational apologetics," something to which authorities in the church have resorted far too often.

Second, it bears the authority that can only come from those who have "been there" as opposed to those who merely observe a belief system from the outside.

Third and finally, it offers a supernatural answer to a supernatural problem. Many of those who delve into Wicca and witchcraft do so because they have witnessed a sad lack of supernatural reality in traditional Christianity. In this book S.A. Tower shows that counterfeit spirituality is greatly inferior to the real.

This is a great teaching tool for Christians, but more importantly, it is a great salvation tool that will help us reach those who have lost their way in the maze of false religion.

~ **Mike Shreve**,
Pastor, Evangelist and
Author of *In Search of the True Light*

# FROM THE CRAFT TO CHRIST

## THE ALLURE OF WITCHCRAFT AND THE CHURCH'S RESPONSE

*Featuring the testimonies of twelve former witches*

S. A. TOWER

**From The Craft To Christ**

Copyright © 2014, 2019 by S. A. Tower

Visit the author's website at www.ex-witch.com

Published by Dwell Publishing LLC,
dwellpublishing@gmail.com

Printed in the United States of America

All rights reserved. This book or parts thereof may not be reproduced in any form, stored in a retrieval system, or transmitted to any form by any means – electronic, mechanical, photocopy, recording, or otherwise – without prior written permission of the publisher, except as provided by United States of America copyright law.

ISBN: 978-0-9849523-4-2 (paperback)

Unless otherwise indicated Scripture is taken from the New King James Version of the Bible. Copyright © 1979, 1980, 1982 by Thomas Nelson, Inc. publishers.

Scripture marked KJV is taken from the King James Version of the Bible.

Scripture marked NASB is taken from the New American Standard Version of the Bible, Copyright © 1973, 1978, 1984 by the Lockmen Foundation.

To protect the privacy of some individuals referred to, names of persons, places, and some other details, have in some cases been changed.

The views and opinions expressed in this book do not necessarily represent the views of the publisher/author. Dwell Publishing LLC/its editors/author/endorsers are not responsible for any of the content provided by the interviewee of the testimonies published.

Cover design by David Munoz Art

Parental discretion is advised.

> "To open their eyes, in order to turn them from darkness to light, and from the power of Satan to God"
>
> ~ Acts 26:18

# CONTENTS

Foreword by Mike Morton ................................................................. xi
Acknowledgments .............................................................................. xiii
Introduction ......................................................................................... xv

Part I: Witchcraft From The Inside... Out

1. Why Wicca? .................................................................................. 21
2. Defining Witchcraft ..................................................................... 33
3. Stirring The Cauldron ................................................................. 43
4. Church Inflicted Wounds ............................................................ 55
5. The Church's Response ............................................................... 63
6. Witchcraft In The Church .......................................................... 73
7. Witnessing To The Witch ........................................................... 95

Part II: New Creations In Christ... Former Witch Testimonies

8. Mike Morton ............................................................................... 107
9. Lupe King ................................................................................... 119
10. Selah Ally Tower ........................................................................ 131
11. Victoria Shephard ...................................................................... 145
12. Taryn Viet .................................................................................. 159
13. Ron Harnage .............................................................................. 171
14. Shalom Shick .............................................................................. 183
15. Mark Bishop ............................................................................... 193
16. April Dryburgh .......................................................................... 201
17. Carrie Christian ......................................................................... 209
18. Shari (Hadley) Pruitt ................................................................. 221
19. Bridget Birkner .......................................................................... 237
20. Evidence of Prayer ..................................................................... 245

Appendix: A Letter To A Wiccan ..................................................... 255

# FOREWORD

In 1989, I started the year walking with the Lord, a licensed minister in the Pentecostal Church of God. Many storms of life came upon me, and instead of drawing closer to the Lord, I walked away from Him and into what I knew to be rebellion: embracing the religious worship and practices of witchcraft. At first I trained and was initiated into the Craft, and over the next twenty years I worked with The Church and School of Wicca as a solitary practitioner, with the Blue Star Tradition, and finally the Black Forest Clan under whom I was elevated to a third-degree in traditional British witchcraft. Ultimately, I was a clan head for Massachusetts and running two covens there. And then in 2009, the Lord miraculously called me out.

I have read a lot of books, testimonies, and accounts of people who claimed to have been witches, but for those who have actually been in the Craft, there are certain words and phrases that are properly used and descriptions of events that either give the story credibility (as in S. A. Tower's first book, *Taken from the Night: A Witch's Encounter with God*) or prove it to be fluff that many Christians unknowingly try to use to share the gospel with those involved in the occult. In the latter case, the lack of credibility serves only as an embarrassment of misinformation and understanding. S. A. Tower has truly been there, and anyone who was or is in the Craft will recognize that when reading her book, as the authenticity and credibility of her personal story continues to the last page.

Today, even high schools and colleges often have their own covens or Wiccan groups, and books on witchcraft and the occult fill the bookshelves in bookstores and libraries across the country. The current media portrays witchcraft as one of the fastest-growing religious movements in America, attracting young and old alike.

However, there is also a mass exodus happening that attracts far less attention. This exodus is not because of disillusionment, but because God is moving in mighty ways to bring people out of witchcraft and other occult activities. From the Craft to Christ, compiled by S. A. Tower, features a collection of such stories of those who have left witchcraft behind and turned to Christ. This much-needed book offers a behind-the-scenes glimpse of both the church's response to those bound under the allure of witchcraft and its subtle influences infiltrating the church today.

I am blessed to know Selah. Her story parallels mine in many ways, as it does so many others whose journey from Wicca to Christ are recounted in this book. Some, like me, once walked faithfully and had turned away from the Christian faith, only to be wooed back by the gentle love, mercy, and grace of the Lord. You will find these true accounts powerful and compelling as each person has a unique story to tell based on their experiences, weaknesses, and vulnerability.

I ask that you take the time to read this book carefully and prayerfully, as I believe its content is essential in understanding the seductive draw of witchcraft and ministering to those involved in the occult. It offers hope that others like us may be brought from eternal darkness into everlasting life.

Now, let's begin to read their stories together

Mike Morton
Former Witch

# ACKNOWLEDGMENTS

First and foremost I am eternally grateful to God for His transforming power that not only rewrote the pages of my life but also the lives of those in this book.

To my family, thank you for your patience during my seemingly endless hours glued to the computer screen, and for the welcomed "joy breaks" loaded with giggles and hugs from our precious little ones.

I would like to express my sincere gratitude to Mike, Lupe, Victoria, Taryn, Ron, Shalom, Mark, April, Carrie, Shari, and Bridget for sharing their inspiring testimonies and insightful quotations, all of which have contributed in making this book a passionate tribute to God. To each of you, my heartfelt thanks.

I am sincerely appreciative of Mike Morton for writing the foreword and sharing his vision of the mass exodus occurring at this time. Your knowledge of the Craft and of Christ is so instrumental in this hour.

This book would not have been possible without the support of my partner-in-crime, Robert from Dwell Publishing. You were the inspiration behind my writing this book. Thank you for helping take it from concept to reality.

A sincere thank you to Muzzie, Doug, Robert, Charles, Pastor K, Durwin, and Stephen for testifying to the power your prayers had in the lives of those mentioned in this book.

To Alex Murashko Jr., thank you for being an inspiration and for providing me the opportunity to share with the world what God has placed on my heart.

A special thank you to Cookie. Words cannot express my sincere gratitude for your generosity and step of faith. May God richly bless you!

To my editors—Larry, Christy, and all those who shared their input—thank you for taking a diamond in the rough and making it shine.

I have truly been blessed with my on-call PC techs who are always quick to get my computer up and running so I can get back to writing. Thanks a million, guys!

# INTRODUCTION

Paul stood on the Areopagus (Mars Hill), overlooking a city given over to idols, and addressed the pagan Athenians. What's striking is that Paul recognized their altar of an unknown god and through it, revealed the one true God. Perhaps even more amazing was that he did so without ever quoting Scripture; in fact, he described God through a pagan poet. He didn't destroy their stone images, call down judgment, or flee from among them; rather, he introduced them to the God they did not know.

What if we talked to the "Athenians" of our era and simply revealed "God" to them? Rather than degrading the gods they worship or condemning these people for worshiping them, as our means of evangelism, what if we were able to demonstrate God to them in ways they could understand? Paul addressed his audience with respectful language yet never endorsed their view of God; he found common ground to describe the God who created the world and everything in it.

If we are going to be able to reach pagans in our generation, we need to do so with an approach similar to the one Paul used at Areopagus. We cannot just quote Scripture and expect people to follow them. As Paul did, we need to learn about their culture, beliefs, and worldview, and then respectfully present the gospel message to them. It is for this very reason that *From The Craft To Christ* was written.

## Doormen for Christ

During my pagan years, my friend Bo agonized over finding a way to best reveal God to me. He pursued an exhausting search to find someone I could relate to, finally tracking down Lupe King, a former Witch who led The Way Out Ministries. At the time, those coming out of the Craft seemed few and far between, but through various social media outlets we uncovered a mass exodus of sorts. We began to meet with those who were leaving, recounting similar stories of how the miraculous love of God manifested in their lives. I was working on my first book, *Taken From The Night: A Witch's Encounter With God*, when Bo came up with the inspirational concept for what would become this book. So I began saving the accounts people shared. Through my own life and the lives of others, I have come to discover that God is reaching out to those who are not always necessarily seeking Him and, in turn, opening their hardened hearts to the God they only thought they knew.

We are just the doormen to invite them to enter in.

## A Double Portion

This book is divided in two parts. The first part is a ministry tool aimed at teaching individuals, as well as the church as a whole, in much the same way that Paul familiarized himself with the Athenian pagans. Within these pages, you will find the answer to the most perplexing question Christians have: Why would anyone choose to be a witch? It provides an insider's view into witchcraft and its practices and, perhaps more importantly, identifies what it isn't and examines the church's response in light of Christ-centered evangelism. Included are quotes from those who bear witness by their own accounts described in this book. I'm excited to introduce you to them: Mike Morton, Lupe King, Victoria Shephard, Taryn Viet, Ron Harnage, Shalom Shick, Mark Bishop, April Dryburgh, Carrie Christian, Shari Pruitt, and Bridget Birkner.

In the second part of the book, readers will learn the individual stories of myself, as well as these eleven former witches who came from various degrees in the Craft, from high priest and high priestesses with over thirty years involvement, down to solitary practitioner. We revisit our early interactions with the church and the pivotal moments the Enemy led us astray. More importantly, this part allows the reader to witness the enormous love of God and His redeeming grace exhibited in each of our lives.

## Let God... be God!

We see increasing in-roads being paved by various beliefs, including New Age philosophies and traditional paganism, into our culture today. Unfortunately, the church's response to those who know little to nothing of our God, is to either reject and condemn them or (strangely) incorporate their practices within our own church walls. Paul left us an insightful paradigm during his visit to the heart of a pagan mecca: he spoke in a way they could relate to but without accepting their belief of God.

We find perversion seeping into many of our churches today. Practices that are clearly of pagan origin are being incorporated into Christian worship services, all to enable a marketable Christianity to a growing universalist society. Many people are enticed by a "feel-good" message and thereby conform. Conversely, although the apostle Paul spoke in a language the Athenians could relate to, his words remained steadfast to the true gospel of Christ. In the end, we find that many scoffed at Paul's message and only a few were saved. Some claim that his message was a failure, but how can we write off the lives that were saved? It seems, even today, we are still looking for numbers rather than relationships with God as the basis for what we consider "success" when it comes to sharing the gospel with the lost.

Through this book, I hope to encourage you to look beyond the unmoved hearts of those involved with Wicca and New Age philosophies, and envision the searching hearts that are willing to ponder the gospel message if only granted the opportunity to do so in a nonjudgmental environment. It is my attempt to convey the essential need for Christians to discern the hearer's heart before butting heads in a theological debate, and instead preach the good news in a way the hearer can receive.

We must adhere to the Great Commission and bring the fullness of the gospel to the unbeliever, whomever they may be, and leave the rest to the Holy Spirit. All too often, we think we have been called to convince or coerce the lost into the kingdom, when Jesus said for us to go and tell (Matthew 28:16–20). Paul led the example on Mars Hill. When he was done preaching, he left them. This is a valuable lesson for the church, to know when to move on and let God ... be God. It's not about the multitudes accepting the message, but rather the message being told to the multitudes and rejoicing in the one life saved.

It is my prayer that after you read this book and the testimonies that declare His glory, you will experience a passion motivated by the love of God to see His power and goodness revealed in the darkness of this age.

– Selah Ally Tower

# PART I

*Witchcraft from the Inside ... Out*

# CHAPTER ONE

## Why Wicca?

The tone of her voice said it all. It was somewhere between utter disgust and sheer shock. One thing was for sure: I had appalled my spiritual mother with what I had just openly confessed. Joan was an intercessor, gifted in discernment, and while she often wore her heart on her sleeve, she saw things strictly as black and white. The bombshell I dropped was met with opposition. How dare I cross over to the side of the Enemy!

I clearly remember the question hurled back at me: "Why would someone who knows the Lord choose witchcraft?" There was nothing I could say that would lighten the mood, because in her mind I had just thumbed my nose at her, the church, and God.

At the time, I was offended by her confrontational tone, which seemed more like an insult than a sincere inquiry. Yet, Christians particularly have serious concerns when it comes to witchcraft that is mostly a knee-jerk response. The word *witchcraft* sends shivers down the spines of many, and sets others off into a merciless rage. Many fear that any association with a practitioner subjects them to demonization, while others pass it off as pure fantasy.

So what is the truth behind this modern yet age-old religion—and why would anyone follow it?

I recently ran across a multi-faith portal on the internet

called Patheos, which offered a Blogger Challenge called "Why I am a ..."[1] In two hundred words or less, contributors of various faiths summarize the reasons for following their particular beliefs. Since I was writing this chapter, I read what bloggers were saying and have included a few examples, which I believe help sum up why they chose Wicca/paganism.

Blogger Yvonne writes, "It's not a faith, it's a practice and a way of life, a way of relating to the world around me with awe and love and wonder and joy."[2] Jason blogs his response, "Paganism offers me the opportunity to interact with the gods in ways that work for me."[3]

We can view witchcraft as a personal form of spirituality that caters to the individual's needs and/or desires. The reasons for choosing this path are many and are often difficult for Christians to comprehend, so this chapter will attempt to answer the number-one question many have asked: "Why Wicca?"

## Nature-Based Spirituality

> *Most Wiccans are nature-lovers, which is not necessarily a bad thing, but worshiping the creation instead of the Creator is idolatry.*

Witchcraft is a nature-based religion, and it appeals to the age-old desire of getting back to being at one with the earth. Shalom Shick, who practiced Wicca for over twenty years after a bad experience with a church, explains, "It was a beautiful, beautiful religion, beautiful philosophy. I worshiped nature, danced in the moonlight naked, and all that fun stuff."

Most Wiccans are nature-lovers, which is not necessarily a bad thing, but worshiping the creation instead of the Creator is idolatry.

---

1   "Why I am a ...," *Patheos*, https://www.patheos.com/new-visions/topics/why-i-am-a.
2   Yvonne Aburrow, "Why I am a Wiccan," *Patheos*, March 30, 2013, https://www.patheos.com/blogs/sermonsfromthemound/2013/03/why-i-am-a-wiccan/.
3   Jason Mankey, "Why I am a Pagan," *Patheos*, March 28, 2013, https://www.patheos.com/blogs/panmankey/2013/03/why-i-am-a-pagan/.

While some Wiccans may argue they revere nature rather than worship it, former-Witch Shalom Shick says, "The philosophy is monotheistic, believing in an ultimate creative force that is so unknowable that they worship its primary manifestation as polarities; hence breaking down the focus for worship into a god and goddess because female and male are the most sacred of these polarities. They also worship nature, being a manifestation of this."

Lupe King, who had gone from an apprentice to a high priestess in the witchcraft capital of Salem, Massachusetts, offers a similar experience: "Wicca showed me how to incorporate everything into a sense of oneness. It had quite an appeal because it seemed so harmless and so beautiful."

I also can attest that when I first began my search into Wicca, something drew me to the tranquility of becoming one with "the All" of nature and part of the great spiral of life. The concept of every living creature, plant, and animal being part of the oneness intrigued me, and my desire to attune with the earth's rhythm and become one with the All soon became my way of life.

Within each of us lies a God-given desire to return to the intimate relationship we had with our Creator in the garden of Eden. As seventeenth-century creation scientist Blaise Pascal said, "There is a God-shaped vacuum in the heart of every man which cannot be filled by any created thing, but only by God, the Creator made known through Jesus."[4] To focus on creation rather than the loving relationship with the Creator takes our focus off God and puts it on to what is tangible to man. This subtle shift from God to self is the first step that leads down the slippery slope away from our spiritual Father. We strive for peace on earth and goodwill toward all but are subject to the effects of fallen man on earth.

Life today is far from the simplicity of Eden, where God provided for Adam and Eve's every need and walked with them in the cool of the day. However, even in this paradise an enemy

---

4   Ann Lamont, "Great creation scientist: Blaise Pascal (1623–1662)," *Creation Ministries International*, https://creation.com/great-creation-scientist-blaise-pascal-1623-1662.

lurked nearby waiting to cast doubt, and because of this we now know evil whose presence is evident in every newscast across the globe. Our attempt to return to the garden results in our fallen misconception that we can somehow get there by taking matters into our own hands.

The problem comes when we exercise our God-given free will to satisfy our own selfish ambitions, which has led to not only neglect of the earth that He has entrusted into our care, but also our self-pride that makes us believe we are somehow better than our next-door neighbor. We need not become one with the All of nature; rather, we need to become one with God. In becoming one with God, we become partakers of His divine nature through Christ Jesus, therefore escaping the corruption of this world (2 Peter 1:4).

The beauty of God's creation is evidence of His wondrous works and reason for us to give Him all the glory. All one needs to do is gaze at the setting sun with the sky's colorful pallet, or watch the ocean waves dancing on the rocky shore, to marvel at His spectacular works. Romans 1:20 proclaims, "For since the creation of the world His invisible attributes are clearly seen, being understood by the things that are made, even His eternal power and Godhead, so that they are without excuse."

*"Nature is God's first missionary. Where there is no Bible, there are sparkling stars. Where there are not preachers there are spring times and the beauty of changing seasons. If a person has nothing but nature, then nature is enough to reveal something about God." ~ Max Lucado*

While our Patheos blogger Yvonne describes Wicca as relating to the world in awe, we know that our awe should not be for the glory of creation but rather the Creator. Nature is the evidence of God. Our Creator sculpted a masterpiece and placed it among the stars and planets in the universe. He added an astounding final touch: human life, which He created in His image and called it good.

## Goddess Spirituality

While women have come a long way in both society and religion over the past century, many have suffered at the hands of discrimination in a male-dominant society. I remember as a teenager declaring my strength and invincibility in Helen Reddy's anthem, "I Am Woman." My independence didn't last, however; years later I surrendered control of my life to the authority of both my husband and the church.

In Wicca, the Goddess is emphasized, while the God, her consort, is her equal. Wiccans consider both necessary for proper balance in creation, but the Goddess has preeminence. A fundamental belief in the Wiccan Goddess is that she predates Christianity and is responsible for both creation and life itself. The Goddess is seen in all women, and this encourages women to see the divine within themselves. Women who feel somewhat left out of Christianity or feel it treats them as a lesser vessel often find the Wiccan concept fills their need for a feminine divinity. Wicca teaches that women are strong and their bodies are sacred. Unfortunately, over the centuries many misconceptions of how God sees women have developed. God's view of women differs greatly from what many of us have grown up believing.

One common misconception of the Bible is that woman does not have the same status as man. However, Scripture reveals that God has a high view of woman from the beginning of time. Genesis 1:27 tells us that man was not the only one created in God's image; woman was as well. In fact, Scripture tells us that man alone was not adequate so God created woman to be his helper (Genesis 2:18).

It is interesting that as a Wiccan, I often heard it said the Christian God considered woman to be evil and the embodiment of sin itself. In reality, God placed the blame of the fall on both Adam and Eve as one flesh; they both disobeyed and suffered the consequences of their actions. It is also interesting to note the name by which God first identified Himself to Abraham: El

Shaddai, meaning "All-Sufficient One"—mighty to nourish, satisfy, and protect. He was (and is) a God who nurtures and cares for His new creation, mankind. Therefore, both female and male attributes dwell within God.

In my attempt to be a godly wife, I submitted to my husband as the king, priest, and prophet of our home. That was a title too heavy for him to bear, and one that brought needless suffering for not only me but also our children. My reliance on a broken man to fulfill his supposed God-given role, rather than reliance on God Himself, is what failed me. At that pivotal and vulnerable moment, the charm of a religion that emphasized feminine divinity over male-dominant spirituality was appealing. Wicca, having a goddess foundation, seemed the perfect alternative.

For Lupe, the concept of a man as the spiritual head of household was unthinkable: "It is hard for a person like me, who has fought her whole life and always been in control ... to believe any man could be superior because the men in my life have been poor examples." On the contrary, Shalom reflects how having grown up with the absence of a male figure altogether, paved the way for goddess spirituality: "When offered a female/goddess to worship, it was relatively easy to follow along since a mother was all I had known. Ultimately, however, it was hollow and frustrating, simply because she was the wrong 'god' and had no real power. And thinking I was a goddess was even more frustrating since humans make inadequate, weak gods."

### Empowerment

For those whose life circumstances rage out of control, a strong desire for change leads many to explore witchcraft and the use of psychic power to take charge of their life. In Wicca, power is invoked through the God and Goddess and/or magick, and that energy is said to flow into the universe to bring about the desired change.

I can attest that many young people drawn to Wicca are intelligent but often bullied, disenfranchised, or shy, and they find personal strength and self-esteem in this all-embracing religion.

The desire can be as simple as making personal changes in order to alter the course of action in one's life or to banish something negative and thus set one free from harm. Though this desire for power appears innocent enough—after all, what could (seemingly) be harmful in changing oneself or their life-circumstance for the better?—the problem lies in seeking empowerment from within.

Lupe explains, "Power, love, and healing as a witch starts out as being goddess oriented. But as time goes on as a witch, you come to realize that you are the God or the Goddess." Wicca teaches that we are all part of the God and Goddess; therefore, we have "the divine within." Thus the power evoked is self-seeking and ultimately renders one defenseless in the face of the Adversary.

> *"Power, love, and healing as a witch starts out as being goddess oriented. But as time goes on, as a witch you come to realize that you are the God or the Goddess." ~ Lupe King*

For others, the allure comes from the powers harnessed in witchcraft, as explained by Mike Morton, who was a high priest for twenty years: "I had tinkered with it as a young teen and was fascinated by the power it supposedly could give you. However, as a teen, I didn't have the discipline or concentration to make it work. In college I came to Christ and got saved. But things in my life imploded when I was a Pentecostal Church of God minister. Instead of drawing closer to the Lord, I blamed Him, rebelled, and reverted back to witchcraft." Mike is one of many who chose witchcraft as an alternative source to reclaim the power within to bring their own desired change.

A former Wiccan practitioner from Africa used magick as a way to gain control over her life and to seek revenge against an abusive stepfather. Taryn Viet explains, "The reason I chose to go the route of Wicca was because I was looking for something with power."

In my life, I grew weary of trying to do what was good and felt as though God had abandoned me and turned a deaf ear. I felt the need to take things into my own hands since in my mind no one else had my best interest at heart. I too knew deep inside that I was rebelling, but I now doubted God's Word. Like Eve, I bit into the fruit of forbidden knowledge, believing at the time that God had kept me from receiving the power to change the devastating circumstances in my life.

It is important to note that any attempt to exercise power to change our lives outside of the will of God ultimately introduces our own will; thus we become our own god/goddess, and most often the result is an unfavorable outcome in the long run. Our desire should be to rest in the center of God's will, recognizing He has the power to change us and our life circumstances from the inside out.

## Spirit-World Communication

The desire for knowledge of the supernatural is nothing new to man; from the beginning man has been in pursuit of it. While none can lay claim in being all knowledgeable, the quest to prove the supernatural continues. Our curiosity of the unknown is evident by the movies and television shows we watch, the videos we play, the books we read, and the psychic fairs we attend.

Reading one's own future by use of tarot cards or other forms of divination are commonplace in Wicca and other forms of paganism, but God forbids them in both the Jewish and Christian faith. Still, we find some Christians who seek supernatural revelation through these mediums, and further evaluation reveals that they are intrigued by the paranormal, perhaps because they have either failed to or been forbidden to seek the supernatural in God.

With this vulnerability comes the desupernaturalization of the church where those in leadership are more interested in structure and order, therefore stifling the movement of the Holy Spirit among the people. My former pastor, John, once explained that the early church spent the first three hundred years without the weekly regiment of a pastor's Sunday morning sermon. He then posed the question, "How, then, did they so strongly impact the world to the point of turning it upside down? It was the moving of the Holy Spirit through those walking in their anointing that empowered the early Christians. The Spirit of God is uncontainable, like the wind that blows where it wills. Afraid of losing control, the institutional church quietly nudged God's active agent out from among us. Mostly, we now have a church made in our image. We worship God based on what we want Him to be like and not who He truly is."

Communication with the spirit world provides yet another attraction to Wicca. While Wiccans believe in the paranormal, many Christian churches either ignore the supernatural or reject it altogether. Many times, a person would end up facing criticism by church leaders, as did Ron Harnage, who had grown up in a home that regularly encountered paranormal activity. However, his church disregarded these disturbances, insisting they were a figment of his imagination or even a result of mental illness.

Ron says, "I knew there must be some explanation, and what began really as a skeptical approach at disproving the supernatural, led into a deeper and deeper involvement in the occult." In Ron's case, his supernatural experience was undeniable, but his church, which could have shed light on these unsolved mysteries, turned a blind eye, leaving him to seek answers elsewhere.

In the article "New Research Explores Teenage Views and Behavior Regarding the Supernatural," David Kinnaman of The Barna Group and Mark Matlock of Wisdom Works Ministries explored many dimensions of teens and their interactions with unexplainable events. They concluded, "It is no wonder most teens believe in the supernatural realm: many have had experiences that could only be described as supernatural or spiritual. For instance, seven million teens have encountered an angel, demon, or some other supernatural being. More than two million teens say they have communicated with a dead person (10%). Nearly two million youth claim they have psychic powers."[5]

---

5 "New Research Explores Teenage Views and Behavior Regarding the Supernatural," Barna, January 23, 2006, https://www.barna.com/research/new-research-explores-teenage-views-and-behavior-regarding-the-supernatural/.

The church considered Lupe "different" as a child because she saw things before they happened and developed sensitivity to people's pain. "That is one reason I went into Wicca, because neither I nor our church and even my own family, considered me to be a Christian." Unfortunately, spiritual gifts, which are God-given abilities meant to benefit the body, are often the source of both confusion and controversy among Christians.

Beyond the indifferences of believers, lies are one of the Enemy's biggest tactics in paralyzing God's purpose in our lives. God created us to be interactive with a need for love and belonging, and rejection is a sting to our identity that is long-lasting. God's desire is not for us to experience the consequences of rejection, but for us to see ourselves as He sees us, as the apple of His eye (Psalm 17:8).

> *We serve a supernatural God whose ways are unnatural to man. He communicates to our spirits through His Spirit and provides supernatural signs or manifestations to reveal Himself to us.*

We serve a supernatural God whose ways are unnatural to man. He communicates to our spirits through His Spirit and provides supernatural signs or manifestations to reveal Himself to us. Not everything supernatural is from God, so we are also subject to a counterfeit spiritual realm. With that said, it doesn't mean we should discard the spiritual entirely, but rather we should discern the difference in what is and is not from God.

### Customized Religion

Jason, our Patheos blogger at the beginning of this chapter, gave his reason for being a pagan as interacting with the gods in ways that worked for him, revealing the allure that personalized spirituality has to offer. Witchcraft comprises a variety of traditions and even more options for solitaries, or those who practice outside of a group. Wicca embraces many gods and goddesses and spiritual practices from different cultures, and each witch incorporates the divine into their own belief system. While most Wiccans have a reverence for nature, their lifestyles for living in harmony with it vastly differ.

## Reflection & Action

Either by yourself or in a small group, reflect on these questions.

- What do you think is the main attraction of Wicca for women? For men? How does that attraction tempt a person to follow Wicca and magick instead of the living God?
- What lie did the Enemy (Satan) tell Adam and Eve in the garden of Eden? How is that lie used to tempt individuals into witchcraft today?
- In Wicca, how are women viewed in the eyes of God? How does God truly see a woman?
- What is the source of power used in Wicca? What is the source of power used in the life of a Christian?
- Why do most of the teens in The Barna Group research believe in the supernatural?

Check which action steps below would be appropriate and realistic for you, or you and others, to take (check all that apply):

- [ ] Form a study group in my church to better understand witchcraft and Wicca and develop ways to witness to those involved in Wicca or tempted to explore it.
- [ ] Conduct a research study that focuses on God's view of women compared to the view of women in European goddess worship.
- [ ] In two hundred words or less, write a letter to a Wiccan explaining why you are a Christian.

# FROM THE CRAFT TO CHRIST

# CHAPTER TWO

## Defining Witchcraft

Wicca can be described as "the religion of witchcraft," whereas witchcraft is "the practice." However, not all witches would agree, as some would claim the opposite and say witchcraft is "the religion" and Wicca is "the practice." Therefore, one can practice Wicca without being a witch, just as one can be a witch without following the Wiccan religion.

Sound confusing? There is an old saying that if you ask any three witches about their religion, you will get at least five different answers, and having firsthand experience with this, I have to agree that defining witchcraft is relatively the same.

The objective in this chapter is not to confuse you, but rather give an overview of Wicca, witchcraft, or simply "the Craft," and define witchcraft and briefly describe its beliefs and practices. Some use the terms *Wicca and witchcraft* interchangeably, while others take offense at being associated with one or the other. Many early witches used the term *Wicca* to avoid the negative associations attached to the traditional perception of "witches," as many still do today. Over the years, Wicca has evolved into a more socially acceptable belief system, and as it does, more people lay claim to its practice.

> *There's an old saying that if you ask any three witches about their religion, you'll get at least five different answers.*

We begin our exploration with Victoria Shephard, a former initiated Witch and freelance writer with several notable articles in pagan publications. Victoria offers her definition of Wicca as, "A nature-based religion worshiping the God and Goddess by honoring the cycles of nature. Whether Wicca and witchcraft are the same depends on who you ask. I use the terms interchangeably, but I know not everyone would. I tend to use the term *Wicca*, as saying you practice 'witchcraft' only produces shock."

Often, the association of these terms are ambiguous even within the pagan community, as described by Mike: "Much of the witchcraft and Wiccan community itself is fluid and hard to define. These terms enjoy a lot of usage with very little discretion. I believe that in some ways they definitely are the same, and in some ways they are not. They are alike in that they share a belief in the ancient gods and goddesses."

With the advancement of technology and the internet, the difference between Wicca and witchcraft has in one way become more defined although Wicca has become more diluted. Ron elaborates, "Wicca and witchcraft are not different, because Wicca is a tradition of witchcraft, but there are many types of cultural witchcraft traditions. When I was a witch, there was a set definition of Wicca, but Wicca has changed somewhat over the years due to the universal movement and also due to the internet making it possible for people to do thorough historical research. Originally, in its modern context it was defined as a Celtic witchcraft tradition, but now it has changed its stance and presents itself as an offshoot of Hinduism based on Tantric yoga."

To further complicate things, many practitioners define themselves as "pagan," which is an umbrella term used to describe various non-Christian traditions.

## Brief History of Wicca

Wicca is a diverse spiritual path, based on living in harmony with nature, that developed between the nineteenth and twentieth centuries. While we can trace its roots to witchcraft, it quickly evolved from elements of many cultural traditions such as Hinduism, Egyptian and European goddess worship, and Shamanism, just to name a few from a seemingly endless list. The word *Wicca* has different origins, depending on who you ask. Some say it comes from an old English word for "wise" or "wise one." Others say it was the word *wica* that Gerald Gardner, a part of a British coven and most notably known as the founder of Wicca, used to call witches of the Craft. Most agree that although its origins began in Europe, it was Raymond Buckland who introduced what is now called the Gardnerian tradition of witchcraft to America around 1964.

Wicca has three major sects, as explained by Ron: "[These include] the old-school original Gardnerian Wicca (described above), Alexandrian witchcraft founded by Alex Sanders, and the Church of Wicca founded by Gavin and Yvonne Frost. These days there are many sub-sects and branches, including Neo-pagans, but they all originate from these three sects." He concludes, "Wicca was born out of the 'Celtic Revival.' The early witches largely borrowed rites and practices from Freemasonry and the Kabbalah, and mixed in other occult traditions as well."

## Wicca's Basic Belief and Practices

Wicca is a religion that worships both male and female aspects of deity (the God and the Goddess), although the Goddess is emphasized more. Wiccan practitioners may be monotheistic, honoring one divine male or female who is often viewed as a facet of a greater godhead, therefore being pantheistic (i.e., seeing all things as part of the God and Goddess, and the earth as a living organism in which all its inhabitants are one). Practitioners may also be polytheistic, worshiping many gods and goddesses equally.

Mike furthers our insight into the worship of the gods: "The worship of various gods and goddesses goes back to the days of Noah, when after the flood, his son's descendants repopulated the earth. One of his great-grandsons, Nimrod, established an empire in the place known as Babylon. He and his wife, Semiramisis, established the earliest mystery religion ... and from this rapidly spreading religion came all the polytheistic and pagan religions. The Goddess was central to this worship; she was, as modern witches proclaim today, known by many names, such as Isis, Astarte, Diana, Hecate, Demeter, Kali, and Rhiannon. The Goddess's consort was also known by multiple names and was divine. In many cases, there was a holy child that was the product of the union of the God and Goddess. This tradition of a female and child was even integrated into the Catholic Church with the veneration of the Madonna and child."

Wicca is an initiatory practice, and initiates are elevated in a degree system within their covens. Solitary Wiccans dedicate themselves, which is committing to follow the Wiccan path.

Wiccans celebrate eight Sabbats, or holidays, in the Wheel of the Year, which mark the beginning and midpoint of seasons. They observe ritual observances called Esbat rites in accordance with the moon's phases, during which they consecrate and cast a circle to create sacred space for the witch or coven to perform rituals.

Reincarnation is a common belief among Wiccans; each considers life on earth a learning lesson in their progression to a higher level of being. Upon death, one does not face judgment, but rather one's spirit goes to a place known as Summerland or Tir 'n' Og or Arianrhod's spiral castle (depending on tradition). Each of these is a sort of heaven where people reunite with old friends and loved ones before returning to earth once again. In stark contrast, the Bible states that man dies once and afterward comes judgment (Hebrews 9:27).

Wicca is more than a religion; it is a way of life. Many practice Wicca for its spirituality and/or philosophy. For some, just living the Wiccan way is enough, while others incorporate witchcraft (the practice of magick) into their belief. Wiccans who practice magick use the energy of nature to influence the world around them, while most avoid the use of black magick (malevolent magick used to harm or manipulate another person's will). To accomplish their goal, they use methods of meditation, visualization, and spells. However, witchcraft isn't inherently Wiccan;

rather, it is the manipulation of energy to bring about change. Witches, as you will soon learn, may practice any religion.

There are numerous Wiccan traditions, just as there are many denominations in Christianity. Some traditions are named after the founder of that tradition, such as Gardnerian named for Gerald Gardner and the Alexandrian tradition named for both its founder Alex Sanders and the Ancient Library of Alexandria. Other traditions are named for their cultural basis, such as Celtic, Teutonic, and Strega, to name a few. In Eclectic Wicca, an individual or coven follows no particular tradition and instead derives their studies from many magickal systems. Overall, Wicca is an individualistic religion practiced not only by covens but by many solitary practitioners, thus making it nearly impossible to differentiate between or list all of the various traditions.

Unlike Christianity and mainstream religions that have denominations overseen by a structured governing body, within Wicca there is no central organization that speaks for all Wiccans or traditions. Wiccans abide by two basic principles known as the Wiccan Rede: "An' ye harm none, do what ye will," and the Three-fold Law: "For what we do for good or for ill, shall be returned to us three-fold." Since Wiccans have no Bible to live by, they hold their moral and ethical conduct by only these two standards.

## Wicca Today

Over the years, Wicca has progressed from a religion practiced in secret, to one that's come out of the broom closet and onto the global stage filled with internet-taught cyber solitaries. Online witch schools offer a considerable number of classes and much information pertaining to Wicca and magick but deeply lack hands-on experience. As a result, its students often fall into an internet melting pot that can only further dilute the traditional Craft.

Christians may think any amount of dilution would be favorable, but I caution that magick in any form, especially in the hands of the untrained, can prove disastrous. In a generation that thrives on instant gratification at the push of a button, many of the original practices of Wicca are being reinvented or eliminated. One founder of The Church and School of Wicca expresses his own concern in the PaganNews.com: "Today (at least in our opinion) the instant-gratification society has led to a lot of self-styled Wiccans who know very little about the underlying philosophical beliefs of the Craft and are not dedicated to the Craft."[6]

> *Many authors and news media sources continue to report a rise in the number of Wiccans today, but I believe it is rather the result of a new microwave version of Wicca and not of those dedicated to the traditional Craft.*

Many authors and news media sources continue to report a rise in the number of Wiccans today, but I believe it is rather the result of a new microwave version of Wicca and not of those dedicated to the traditional Craft. The original Craft required time (at least a year and a day), study, and practice. It takes a lot of commitment and hard work, whereas today's Wicca may include an online course and initiation in just a few short months to conform to the current generation's demands for instantaneous results with little to no effort. Today's youth quickly lose interest in anything other than religion-on-demand, including Wicca.

That is not to say that the original traditions of Wicca are no longer in existence, but rather that the rise of its followers is not nearly as high as many perceive it to be. Wicca continues to evolve as it progresses, weaving into a changing society, thus breaking its own traditions in the process and ultimately altering its beliefs and practices.

## What Wicca Is Not

The first definition most Christians would give of Wiccans is that they are Satan worshipers. Here is where the devil is in the details. Wiccans do not believe Satan exists, except perhaps in

---

6   Gavin and Yvonne Frost, "Applying Traditional Therapies, Rituals and Systems," *Pagan News*, http://www.pagannews.com/gyf.shtml.

the minds of Christians. Since they don't believe in the existence of the devil, they do not believe they are worshiping him. It is thought by many Wiccans that one would have to be a Christian before they could be a Satanist.

Satanism can be either atheistic (where practitioners view Satan as a symbol of rebellion) or theistic (where practitioners believe in Satan as a spiritual being). Both of these types of Satanism are left-hand (malicious black magick) paths, whereas Wicca is considered a right-hand (benevolent white magick) path.

*The first definition most Christians would give of Wiccans is that they are Satan worshipers. Here is where the devil is in the details. Witches do not believe Satan exists, except perhaps in the minds of Christians.*

## Traditional Witchcraft and Pre-Wicca Craft

There are numerous pre-Wicca traditions of witchcraft, and most claim a much older historical origin than Wicca and Christianity, with roots based in European practices. Some even claim this ancient practice dates back to prehistoric times. While this would be hard to prove, we can certainly trace witchcraft back to the Old Testament. However, what exactly its practices were back then and how closely it resembles witchcraft today remains uncertain. Its philosophy is in natural magick, which seeks knowledge and understanding to achieve living in harmony with all natural forces.

Traditional witchcraft is neither a religion nor a belief system, and while it may have spiritual overtones, it does not necessarily follow a deity. Witches may honor the gods, however their reverence is to nature and the spirits of the land. Most of what we have learned about witchcraft has come from historians and anthropologists. Some witches follow a folklore tradition handed down by word of mouth or secret Grimoires (books of magick) through generations, and most are not in published works. Witchcraft is polytheistic, meaning all spirits, gods, and animal spirits are viewed as part of "the One," therefore worship is unnecessary. While the witch may create their own path, the core belief is rooted in the knowledge and use of magick.

Initiation in witchcraft has no set time frame such as in Wicca, and in fact, it may take many years. The witch must first gain knowledge and complete a specific task before initiation is possible. Unlike in Wicca, there are no further degrees in witchcraft. The Sabbats celebrated correspond with agricultural seasonal cycles, and Esbats are the same as in Wicca and coincide with moon phases. Most believe that when a person dies, they return to the land and become one with or are reunited with the land spirits.

## Witchcraft, the Magick Art

Witchcraft is the craft of the witch. The witch practices magick by use of energy manipulation, causing change by using the power within and natural energies such as those of trees, plants, crystals, stones, and herbs. Witchcraft utilizes spirit-world communication to effect change in our mundane world. Magick is seen as neither good nor evil; rather, it is considered a neutral force, therefore witchcraft is looked upon as a morally neutral practice.

A witch, then, is best described as an individual who practices the art of magick. To the witch, magick is a way of life, so it is often spontaneous. The most powerful tools used in magick is the mind and will power. There is no need for a circle or sacred boundary for working magick, as witches believe the earth to be sacred; therefore the witch seeks a place outdoors where they feel a connection. For many, this interaction with the earth, the land, and the cosmos, along with the ritual acknowledgment of the agriculture seasonal cycles, is the essence of their Craft. In times of old, the witch was the wise woman who usually lived on the edge of town and whom villagers consulted for potions and spells.

Unlike Wiccans, witches do not live by the Rede or Three-fold Law. Therefore, any form of magick, be it creative or destructive, is not off limits. Witches are taught to be responsible for their actions in their use of magick, but since witchcraft is considered neutral, it can encompass both spells and hexes, and ultimately comes down to the intent of the witch. Witchcraft can be described as a series of physical actions and/or rituals performed to achieve a specific end result. Since witchcraft is a magick art, any person, religious or otherwise, may practice it.

## Luciferianism

Luciferianism is similar to Satanism in that they both hold left-hand path philosophies. Some people claim it is an offshoot of Wicca with an emphasis on Satanism, however the interpretation of Lucifer is in complete opposition since Wicca doesn't acknowledge Satan in any form. Others would argue it is an altogether separate belief system.

Carrie Christian, a former Eclectic Witch who also incorporated Luciferianism in her form of witchcraft, provides insight: "Lucifer is looked upon as the 'shining one,' bearer of light, and more commonly, the morning star. Some look upon him as a deity to be worshiped, while others see him as a mere symbolism to be followed. "Not all use ceremonial rituals to worship, but others will be ritualistic in their practice. There are no set rules that state whether one way or the other is definitive, as it's more of a personal preference. Luciferians do not see their worship or acts as being rebellious, but as a furtherance of self-enlightenment."

Not surprisingly, Luciferians don't believe in heaven or hell, and rather seek to experience the here-and-now. Since Luciferianism is regarded a belief rather than a religion, there are some witches who incorporate some aspects of Luciferianism into their practice.

## Reflection & Action

Either by yourself or in a small group, reflect on these questions.

- Why is it difficult to give a clear-cut definition of Wicca/witchcraft?

- The Old English word *wicca* meant "wise" or "wise one." What did Gerald Gardner's use of the word refer to?
- Who established the earliest mystery religion? What significance did that have on modern witches today?
- What law do Wiccans follow? How does it compare to the Bible?
- From a witch's point of view, what qualification must one have to be a Satanist?
- What is the oldest biblical reference to the existence of witches and their prohibited practices?
- In your opinion, are witchcraft and Wicca the same? Different? Explain.

Check which of the action steps below would be appropriate and realistic for you, or you and others, to take (check all that apply):

☐ Research Jesus' encounters with witches and sorcerers and describe how He responded.

☐ Through prayer, soul-search and define any hidden idolatry or practices not of God in your own life.

☐ List any pagans you know or that God has placed on your heart and commit to pray for them consistently.

# CHAPTER THREE

—⚯—

## Stirring the Cauldron

Every October, Facebook is ablaze with condemning posts by Christians debating Halloween—so much so that I have dedicated a chapter to this highly contested holiday.

Out of the eight holidays celebrated by witches and Wiccans, Samhain (pronounced sow-in) stands out as the most controversial for Christians because it is often associated with Halloween. It has been the target of much debate and condemnation between those who celebrate and those who forbid its practice. Some Christians concerned with its origins and practices avoid participation while others modify what traditions they incorporate. But what are the real concerns about this holiday, and what do witches really do on this particular night of the year?

### Halloween vs. Samhain

It is interesting to note that the Catholic Church lays claim to the origins of Halloween. April Dryburgh conveys the insight her priest shared with her after she returned to church: "When I identified as a pagan, I thought (because I was told and believed it) that Halloween was strictly pagan. After returning to church, accepting Christ, and discussing it with a priest, I have learned that this is not entirely true. All Saint's Day, an official holiday of the Catholic Church, is the day after All Hallows' Eve (what has now become Halloween)." All Saints Day (November 1), according to the Catholic Church, is a day to commemorate those martyred for their faith, whereas All Souls Day (November 2) is a time set aside to pray for the departed souls held in purgatory.

> You will hear some witches and other Neo-pagans claim that Halloween is nothing more than a Christianized version of Samhain—a stolen holiday of sorts, much like every other Christian holiday such as Christmas and Easter.

You will hear some witches and other Neo-pagans claim Halloween is nothing more than a Christianized version of Samhain—a stolen holiday of sorts, much like every other Christian holiday such as Christmas and Easter. For instance, most Christians agree that Jesus was likely born in late-September or early October, so why move the celebration of His birthday to December 25? Many believe it was the church's attempt to offer former pagans a substitute for a holiday their new faith was asking them to abandon.

Shalom explains what she was taught during her pagan years: "Halloween is the version of Samhain that was created to allow pagans to continue to practice paganism under a Christian cover. I knew this when I was practicing Wicca and found it very amusing knowing Christians were celebrating pagan holy days unknowingly."

Many Christians also agree with this theory and apply biblical principles to the bits and pieces of what they know of these ancient practices. For those who share this view, there is a common agreement in the avoidance of any association with this holiday. Shalom explains, "But it is still difficult to communicate these truths to believers comfortable with the traditions of men. It is very important to realize that our Father has warned against worship that uses the traditions of worship to other gods. He is clear about this in Deuteronomy 18:9."

However, not all ex-witches see Samhain and Halloween as one and the same. Mike differentiates between the two, "For me, there is a definite difference between Samhain and Halloween. Many Christians too easily blend the two together, and while there is some truth to their argument, there are also a lot of differences between the two." He explains how the importance of Samhain went beyond a pagan event: "It was a date of great importance to not just the Wiccans and pagans of olden times, but also to the general population who were far and large, an agricultural people. Samhain was considered an 'in-between' time, when the veil between the worlds was at its thinnest, a perfect time for divination to predict the coming year."

Mark Bishop, a former Eclectic Witch, explains how timing loosely connects Halloween with Samhain: "Samhain is a multi-faceted time that was historically a series of harvest celebrations throughout Europe. The timing shifted a little with different groups of people as they were in different growing seasons. For those on the magick paths, it is a season where the spiritual realm is easier to access than the rest of the year. This is loosely tied to the time frame around Halloween but does shift in either direction from that day."

Research about both Halloween and Samhain reveals few actual facts, but a lot of speculation. Some say Halloween is rooted in the immigration of the Irish who brought with them many of their folk beliefs and practices which are incorporated in our celebration of this holiday today. Regardless of how it got to the United States, it would seem that Halloween, at least by today's standard, is a mixed brew of practices from Christianity, paganism, and society in general.

> *It would seem that Halloween, at least by today's standard, is a mixed brew of practices from Christian, paganism and society in general.*

From the available research, timing is the main contributing factor that ties the two together. Halloween's and Samhain's actual focuses and practices are considerably different. Neither are mentioned as a celebrated holiday in the Bible, so our conviction would have to come down to actual practices in light of Scripture. Since dressing up is not forbidden in Scripture, a costume party is not out of the question, though one could easily cross the line into divination, which is forbidden in Deuteronomy 18:10, by having tarot cards read.

What exactly is the holiday celebrated by witches? Samhain is the final harvest, known as the "Summer's End" and the beginning of the dark half of the year. It is considered by the witch as a very magickal time when the veil between the world of the living and the world of the dead is thinnest. Its observances include honoring dead loved ones, communicating with the deceased, and predicting the future through divination. Witches also consider it the Celtic New Year, when practitioners transform the somber and benevolent observance of honoring the dead into a time of merry-making.

Victoria offers her opinion from growing up from a secular viewpoint: "Whether Halloween and Samhain are the same is perspective. Since I was not raised in a Christian family, Halloween was about dressing up and going door-to-door for candy. When I grew up, I still dressed up. Only when I became Wiccan, it became my New Year and a time to go to a Reclaiming Halloween ritual in San Francisco."

> *"Perhaps their words are true. Halloween is the worship of a false god. But it's not the gods and goddesses of the witches or pagans, but the God before whom almost every American, whether or not they are Christian, bows their knee, and that is ... money."*
> —Mike Morton

Mike divulges a common misconception concerning the holiday: "A few insist that Samhain was the name of a satanic holiday and that it worshiped a god of death by that name. This was as mistaken as could be, yet it was often said an 'expert' disclosed this on some television program. Again, this was erroneous information and every witch or pagan knew it. A review of the many catalogs and encyclopedias of gods and goddesses as well as documentation available online quickly proves no such god as 'Samhain' ever existed or was worshiped anywhere. Perhaps their words are true. Halloween is the worship of a false god. But it's not the gods and goddesses of the witches or pagans, but the God before whom almost every American, whether or not they are Christian, bows their knee, and that is ... money."

Today, Halloween has evolved into a commercialized holiday where Americans spend an enormous amount of cash on costumes, candy, and decorations. Kids dress up and go door-to-door for treats, which is a blend of both ancient and modern influences. Some modern witches will partake in Halloween for what they consider a cultural holiday and take their kids trick-or-treating alongside other neighborhood kids, including Christians who aren't alarmed by possible pagan roots. Upon arriving home, they will go through the same safety ritual as other parents, inspecting candy and making sure the kids do not overdose on sugar.

Mark shares his view on the commercialization of Halloween: "Halloween, as it is currently practiced, is the candy-makers holiday. In the past it was a celebration in conjunction with All Saints Day, which is where the timing came from. As a cultural barometer, it has made it easier to watch things slide as the influence of the church has waned. The costumes and movies seem to get worse every year ... which is something for the church to ponder and pray about. That aside, Halloween is generally about candy, costumes, and scary stories."

With this in mind, a word of caution is in order for those who allow their children to dress in costume. Putting on a costume can be like temporarily taking on the persona of the character you portray, so use discernment in costume choices. My former pastor, who has been involved in deliverance ministry for years, warned us of a believer who unwittingly became demonically influenced while wearing such a costume.

Many adults see Halloween as a chance to engage in fantasy by dressing in costume, and an excuse to party into the night. Modern-day witches may join them, but ironically, some avoid it along with many Christians. That's right! A good percentage of witches see Halloween as a commercialized parody of what they consider serious and sacred. All the stereotypes throughout the year come to fruition on Halloween, all for the sake of what they consider a Christian holiday.

> A good percentage of witches see Halloween as a commercialized parody of what they consider serious and sacred. All the stereotypes throughout the year come to fruition on Halloween, all for the sake of what they consider a Christian holiday.

As you can see, not all of our former witches are in agreement with Halloween participation. But rather than debate personal convictions, let's consider the actual practices our former witches took part in on Halloween and on Samhain during their years of involvement.

Ron offers his account of a typical Halloween night: "I never really did much on Halloween except entertain a few parties and eat too much candy." He goes onto explain his ordinary Samhain experience, "I usually had some type of ceremony, mostly just working with my spirit guides, but that was about it."

Shalom shares her Samhain experience: "Samhain was my favorite holy day as a Wiccan, though I didn't like the green-faced witches that were displayed at that time of year. When I was the Tennessee representative for the Witches League for Public Awareness, I distributed fliers to local merchants that explained that it was not appropriate to display that sort of thing on a 'legitimate holy day.' And, of course, there were the Sabbat gatherings that I attended with the Cosby and Knoxville, Tennessee, covens."

Mike describes one of his Samhain ritual experiences: "I celebrated Samhain as a sacred festival, and it was the one festival that I always celebrated on the specific date. We performed the normal circle casting, invocations of the quarters, the lord, and lady. The ritual had two parts. One, a simple one ... each person was handed a piece of parchment paper and told to write on it something they wanted to get rid of and something they wanted to receive, and then one by one, the people went to the blazing fireplace and dropped their parchment into the flames. Then we invited anyone who wanted, to bring forward the items they brought in memory of their departed and place it on the table so that they could sit for a few minutes and commune with their loved one. The room was quickly filled with sobs and weeping as one by one they came forward. The circle was opened, and all enjoyed a very hearty feast."

When not participating in a Samhain ritual with his coven, Mike describes the "Dumb Supper" ritual he always performed with his wife: "Dumb, because the guest could not speak. It was based on the belief that our deceased loved ones could come visit us. A table was set, which included a variety of foods, drink, and anything that our loved ones were known to especially enjoy. A tall pillar candle was lit, and the table remained set overnight with the open invitation to our loved ones to come, partake, and know that they were not forgotten."

He further differentiates this with Halloween: "Well, as the Farrars (Wiccan elders) pointed out, when people know you are a witch, they expect you to do something special on Halloween. And so I delighted in handing out candies to trick-or-treaters and doing tarot readings for friends. I definitely did (and still do) consider Samhain to be different from Halloween. Many Christians today cannot and will not differentiate between the two, but they are actually very different."

April explains her participation in a Samhain ritual at an interfaith church: "A couple of times I went to a ritual hosted at a Denver Unitarian Universalist church attended by people of various beliefs but mostly Wiccan. There was socializing and tarot readings, followed by a circle. A pagan priestess led the circle, casting 'protection' first, and then inviting spirits of good will to join us in our circle. We danced around the circle chanting and trying to commune with spirits who had passed on." April shares how she celebrated Halloween at an office party: "There was also an annual Halloween party a few years when I worked at the psychic line. It was people who worked at the psychic line in attendance, but it was mostly drinking and dancing in costume."

Mark shares his insight regarding Halloween: "When I was walking the magick paths, I tended to view Halloween as a time to get cheap candy, as it was just another over-commercialized holiday, much like the hype around Christmas. As far as the Samhain season, that was a time for tighter protections ... and any major workings, if it was convenient then. Otherwise, it was just another season, much like the four temporal seasons of the year."

Personally, I took my own kids out trick-or-treating on Halloween and juggled handing out candy in between. Our coven held an annual Witches' Ball, which was a big event and as elaborate as a wedding, on the weekend nearest Halloween. We held a basic public ritual during the ball, creating sacred space, invoking the God and Goddess, and observing the turn of the wheel in honoring the dead. Ritual concluded with a blazing cauldron outdoors where everyone threw their parchment that listed a habit they wanted to be rid of into the flame, amid drumming, chanting, and shouting.

Our actual Samhain celebration was held quietly on the official day of Samhain in a private coven-only ritual. The ritual was performed in the dark, and we were usually sent out into the cold night to divine our future in a scrying mirror or crystal ball. Our bodies shivered as we stood barefoot on the frozen earth until one by one we came before the Goddess. We welcomed the warmth of the fireplace as we threw our parchment into its flames, visualizing the dissipation of what wanted to be rid of. An ancestral altar held pictures or items of deceased loved ones, and a time was set aside to mediate or commune with them, which could be emotional. After the ritual, we would engage in feasting and merry-making.

Contrary to what you may have thought, there was no mention of the gory stuff often associated with witches and Halloween, such as animal sacrifice or other criminal activity. And that is because those things are not commonly practiced. However, in light of Scripture, there are three major problems with Christians partaking in not only Samhain but all Wiccan Sabbat (holiday) rituals, which are: 1) the worship of other gods (see Exodus

20:2–3); 2) divination, or looking to sources other than God for answers (see 1 Samuel 15:23); and 3) interaction with those who have passed on (see Luke 16:26). Most Halloween activities children engage in would not fall under these categories, but in the event that they do, the same would apply.

## The Satanist and Halloween

The highest holiday for a Satanist is not Halloween, as one would expect, but rather their birthday, as Satanism is a self-centered, indulgent religion. Satanists do not require holiday celebrations, and accordingly there are no specific Halloween rituals, as they hold no ties with ancient practices. Therefore, they are free to celebrate in any manner that suits self.

Former-Witch Carrie Christian provides insight into the Halloween celebration in the satanic coven she was part of: "The satanic coven was more of a sex party, orgy type of celebration. There was blood-letting from each other; it was a requirement for the night, due to it being a life force and taking of someone's body. It was more of a sado-masochistic thing. There was a lot of alcohol and drug use. I would use alcohol as it helped to lower the inhibitions whereas sex was concerned. I will say while I was present at the satanic coven, I saw no human sacrifice."

## Conclusion

As Christians, we are called to bring the good news of the gospel to all tribes and nations. Our churches and their ministries send missionaries all around the globe to evangelize the many who have never heard the gospel and those who worship other gods. We send our missionaries to the mountains of Peru and the villages of Haiti; they walk for miles through the dangerous forest of New Guinea, passing by witch doctors, Voodoo ceremonies, and those practicing black magick.

Though our missionary brothers live in areas plagued with extreme darkness, they don't celebrate local rituals; rather they rejoice in the light of Jesus and the many lives that have changed. When they return to share with the church how our tithes and offerings made it all possible, we hear their inspiring stories of how they connected with the hardened hearts they encountered. We rejoice with them and rightly so. Yet somehow, we stop short of stepping out into the dark streets of America, fearing the alleged dark practices in our own backyard instead of reclaiming the land for the Lord. Concerned by evil influences on Halloween, we hide behind closed doors rather than share our light from open ones.

> In all our efforts to prove Halloween is wicked, or in our futile attempts to substantiate that it is not, we end up missing the true face of evil.

Furthermore, I believe the most troubling of all is when we pass judgment or demonize those whose actions do not line up with ours. In all our efforts to prove Halloween is wicked, or in our futile attempts to substantiate that it is not, we end up missing the true face of evil. The world is watching, and the most impact we can have will not be in trick-or-treating or staying indoors but rather in the way we show the love of Christ to one another and those of the world.

## Reflection & Action

Either by yourself or in a small group, reflect on these questions.

- According to the Catholic Church, what are the origins of Halloween?
- Many Christians and pagans alike are in agreement regarding Halloween's origins. What draws them to the same conclusion?
- What is Samhain? What is the main link between it and Halloween?
- What is the American god of Halloween? Why is it a root of all evil?

- Why is it important to use both common sense and discernment when choosing your child's (or your own) Halloween costume?
- In your opinion, are Halloween and Samhain the same? Different? Explain.

Check which of the action steps below would be appropriate and realistic for you, or you and others, to take (check all that apply):

- [ ] If you and your group are in agreement that Halloween was created by the early church to appease pagans converting to Christianity, discuss why converts would need a substitute for a belief they no longer followed. List what other Christian holidays could fall under this same umbrella.

- [ ] If a majority of your group believes that Halloween and Samhain are two different holidays that happen to fall within a similar time frame, discuss what ways the holidays are similar and in what ways they are different.

# FROM THE CRAFT TO CHRIST

# CHAPTER FOUR

—⋙—

## Church-Inflicted Wounds

Many years ago, one of my then-covenmates shared a story of his turnoff to Christianity that played an instrumental part in his walking away from the faith. He (a new Christian) and a few Christian brothers were in the backyard of a mutual friend's house and came upon a trapped small animal (the owner had set a few traps to catch unwanted wildlife on his property). When these supposed good Christian men found their frightened prey, they kicked, poked, and beat it to death, despite the protest of my friend, as they apparently recited Scripture in their defense that God had given man dominion over animals.

It is heartbreaking to think a lack of understanding of Scripture and man's lack of appreciation of God's creation would cause the death of an innocent animal and the spiritual death of a man's faith. We can argue that it is not reason enough for someone to give up their belief in God over the insensitivity of alleged Christians, but the reality is that it happened.

In Genesis 1:29, God gave humanity dominion over the animals, meaning for us to tend and care for them. Man bears the responsibility to rule over them, not mistreat or abuse them, much in the same manner God rules over us. These Christian men were ignorant regarding God's entrusted care of the animals to man, but it goes even deeper than that. Their action and attitude became a stumbling block to my friend, who to my knowledge has yet to return to the Christian faith. A better understanding of

Scripture and a familiarity of the true nature of God would have saved my friend from walking away from the God who loves him.

## The Bad Church Experience

> *"A righteous man regards the life of his animal, but the tender mercies of the wicked are cruel" (Proverbs 12:10).*

How many non-church-going adults do you know who have bad feelings toward Christianity or, worse yet, are mad at God because of a bad church experience? All too often people are out of fellowship because of an offense by another in the body. But the offense does not always come from a brother or sister; sometimes it comes from an elder or pastor and seeps into church doctrine.

If the avoidance of the church is not concern enough, man seeking to fulfill his God-given spiritual need is. God created us as spiritual beings who naturally seek both communion with God and fellowship with one another, but if there is a gap rather than a bridge of unity, we'll seek another source to fulfill that need. Interestingly, most pagans I have met have a bad taste about Christianity, and many who have walked away from the faith share a common denominator: a bad church experience.

> *"The greatest single cause of atheism in the world today is Christians: who acknowledge Jesus with their lips, walk out the door and deny Him by their lifestyle."*
> —Brennan Manning.

Not all disgruntled Christians turn to paganism. My friend Bo's father had a misunderstanding with the Baptist Church when he was a young man, which was the catalyst of his atheism for the rest of his life. I am not saying that everyone hurt by the church will become a pagan or atheist, or resort to other religions, but it warrants a serious look at their experiences.

## Twisted Scriptures

Victoria was a young girl innocently borrowing a cassette tape from her church library, but the sermon she listened to would condemn her for fifteen years, as she felt hopeless believing she would have to live a sinless life. I am sure if the pastor knew he sent a young girl wandering in the wilderness for years, it would surprise him.

Yet I have to ask: How many empty hearts are still out there in the pews, believing they are beyond hope? Was there no check in place that would prevent a ten-year-old from having access to a sermon meant for the mature-minded? After all, we are not talking about children's church and borrowing a VeggieTales tape. Furthermore, had no one built a rapport with her for spiritual questions or acknowledged her lack of church attendance since?

This does not just pertain to children. Perhaps visitors came to church for the first time and walked out believing God condemned them for all eternity. It seems reasonable to say we should have some level of accountability with the messages we deliver. So am I suggesting a watered-down gospel to avoid offense? Absolutely not. Without the protein of the meat we would fail to grow, but as the church, should we not take responsibility and at least cut the meat into bite-size morsels to make it more digestible and avoid any misunderstanding for the young in spirit?

## Something Supernatural

"The church is so schizophrenic!" Ron quipped. "One minute it's teaching you about the spiritual realm, but then they avoid you like the plague when you encounter it." Ron's story recounts just that. He grew up in a home that experienced demonic activity, but when he sought help from his church, they told him he was crazy. Their denial only led him on a search to prove the existence of the supernatural.

Strangely, that is not uncommon even in some churches today. Pastors preach sermons on topics such as Jesus healing the demoniac man, but then we are told it was strictly done in Jesus' day. Rather than confront our discomfort in the unseen, we sweep it under the carpet or attempt to convince ourselves of some natural means. Since this is strong foundational theology in some denominations, it is difficult for us to expect they will see things differently in the near future.

Setting aside the supernatural debate, we as Christians should reach out to those in need. If your child wakes up with a nightmare, do you tell him he is crazy for believing there are monsters under his bed? Or do you turn on the light and check beneath the bed before praying and tucking him back in for the night? If only Ron's church had taken the demonic seriously and let the light of Jesus reveal the hidden demons, then our friend could have remained in the comfort of his swept-out home. At the very least, could the church not have gathered to pray?

## Baptism of Rejection

You can imagine the "amens" when a young teenage girl gave her life to Christ during the church service, but what happened afterward was a disgrace. Shalom excitedly returned the next night to be baptized, as we encourage all new Christians to do, but the question asked of her by the pastor was not whether she had accepted Jesus as her Lord and Savior but rather if she spoke in tongues.

Not yet having received that gift, she innocently explained that while she had not, she was anxiously awaiting it. The pastor refused to baptize her since she lacked their criteria of speaking in tongues and so she left rejected, vowing never to step foot in church again. This bad church theology sidetracked a fervent believer for years!

It is amazing how many doctrines of the church turn away people who are earnestly searching for God. Had this young woman received the gift of discernment, she likely would have pursued another church to be baptized in. Instead, she went running into the arms of the waiting Enemy with a gift of his own: spiritual bondage. In fact, rejection is one of the most common tactics the Enemy uses to paralyze God's purpose in our lives.

We can describe spiritual rejection as a "spiritual death," and you would think the church would rather teach what it means to be alive in Christ and free from the many faces of rejection. The only requirements for water baptism are a belief in Jesus as your Savior and the decision to make Him the Lord of your life. Few fully understand the changes that profession will bring when they first utter those words. Of course, the profession of one's faith should be preceded by asking God for forgiveness for all sins in their past.

The response to those who ask, "What must we do?" is the same today as it was during Peter's time: "Repent, and let every one of you be baptized in the name of Jesus Christ for the remission of sins; and you shall receive the gift of the Holy Spirit. For the promise is to you and to your children, and to all who are afar off, as many as the Lord our God will call" (Acts 2:38–39).

## Supernatural Outcast

For as long as she can remember, Lupe could feel people's pain and foretell events before they happened. This caused more than a raised eyebrow in both the church and her family, but the final straw came when she was cast out of the church while her father turned a blind eye. One can only fathom the effect on a maturing girl's identity. With no one to train her in using her spiritual gifts, she turned to occult books and magazines for instruction. Once again, we see how spiritual immaturity and poor theology detoured her walk toward God.

*It is amazing how many doctrines of the church turn away people who are earnestly searching for God.*

It is hard to comprehend how a minor could be subject to the excommunication meant for the mature-minded Christian who intentionally rejects God. This can only be explained as an extreme misinterpretation of the disfellowshipping Scripture

(Matthew 18). Though we must acknowledge that not all parents are taught spiritually sound interpretations, it does not minimize that parental rejection is just as devastating and leads to feelings of being unlovable and unworthy. Many who have painful experiences of rejection in childhood, or parental criticism, often develop avoidance behaviors that set the course for the Enemy's destruction later in life.

### Paralyzed in Unbelief

During my early Christian years, "Delight yourself also in the ways of the LORD, and He shall give you the desires of your heart" (Psalm 37:4) was often quoted. My desires were godly ones—to have a marriage and family that glorified God—so I could not understand why after years of prayer and fasting, God had not answered them. Over time, I began to doubt the Word of God as relevant for my life. Doubt turned to unbelief, which was a critical moment for the Enemy. He now had me exactly where he wanted me: paralyzed in my unbelief with a faith that had grown dim.

> "From the beginning Satan lured them in and said, 'Do you think you're really going to die?'"
> —Francis Chan

The twisting of Psalm 34:4 would have an immense impact on my life for years to come. It was one way the Enemy used to create doubt and cause unbelief to take root, which led to my eventual fall. Who would have thought a Scripture shared in church would be used by the Enemy to deceive me into believing God was not honoring His promises and had abandoned me? After all, God said it and if I had not received it, it could not possibly be God, since He did not lie, so that left all the blame on me. Years later, I finally realized that my desire was infringing on my husband's free will, the same God-given free will I had executed in leaving the faith and one that God would not dishonor.

## Conclusion

The above stories come from a few of the former witches who share their testimonies in part two of this book. Not one of them is looking to place blame on their church for their choosing to explore Wicca. One day we will all stand before God, and saying, "The church made me do it," will neither find us favor with God nor gain our entrance into His kingdom.

When faced with adversity, each person must make a personal choice, and one cannot blame their church for pushing them into it, in the same way one cannot blame a coven or pagan group for coercing them into it. But while we accept the responsibility for our choices, we also cannot minimize the reality and impact of the opposing Enemy. If we place fault solely on the church, God, or man, we may overlook the real culprit who "walks about ... seeking whom he may devour" (1 Peter 5:8).

## Reflection & Action

Either by yourself or in a small group, reflect on these questions.

- In Genesis, what did God mean when he said for man to have dominion over all of creation? In what way had the Word been twisted in the example given in this chapter?
- In what way can church doctrine be harmful if not based on biblical truth?
- While churches may not acknowledge the supernatural's existence, how can they better handle a church member's experience with the supernatural?
- What does Psalm 37:4 mean? In my situation described in this chapter, what prevented my desires from being fulfilled?
- In each of the accounts given, did the actions of a church draw the individuals to God or away from God? Why?

- In each of these circumstances, what was the root cause of both the deception and the twisting of God's Word?

Check which of the action steps below would be appropriate and realistic for you, or your and others, to take (check all that apply):

- ☐ Volunteer on your church's tape or CD ministry team, and categorize media that are youth friendly and age appropriate. Discuss with your pastor if an assistant pastor, elder, or the pastor himself may want to include a short introduction and their email address with any sermons that may need additional clarification for new believers.

- ☐ Research what it means to be baptized and any requirements necessary to receive this traditional Christian rite. Then compare your research to see if it matches up with your own church's doctrine.

- ☐ List some of the most misinterpreted Scriptures. Research the correct interpretation for each one.

# CHAPTER FIVE

## The Church's Response

In the previous chapter, we discussed where the church may have become an unintentional tool used by the Enemy to lure seekers into alternative forms of spirituality. In this next chapter, we will review the church's response to those who choose witchcraft over Christianity.

The majority of church leadership draws their conclusions about witches based on the following Scriptures: "Thou shalt not suffer a witch to live" (Exodus 22:18 KJV), and perhaps more mercifully, "There shall not be found among you any one that ... useth divination, or an observer of times, or an enchanter, or a witch. Or a charmer, or a consulter with familiar spirits, or a wizard, or a necromancer. For all that do these things are an abomination unto the LORD" (Deuteronomy 18:10–12 KJV). In my case, the church applied Matthew 18:17, which says that if someone is taken in sin and "refuses even to hear the church, let him be to you like a heathen and a tax collector." Since tax collectors in those days took more than the Romans required, they were not exactly popular with the people of God. Do not get me wrong, I certainly looked the part of a witch, but I had come to church.

Many times, the church's reaction is because of a misinterpretation of Scripture causing them to believe that anyone involved in witchcraft is too far gone for salvation, or there is a hidden fear that even attempting to evangelize a witch can cause the Christian to be pulled into its web. All too often there is a notion that someone has planted the witch in the congregation to manipulate the people into Satan's snare. Somehow, the thought that the Holy Spirit may be what drew the witch to church is the furthest thing from some believers' minds.

## The Uninvited

As a past recipient of church shunning, I can attest to the emotional trauma its effects had on my life. That may seem hard to understand—after all, I had chosen a Wiccan lifestyle over Christianity—but the impact of the social rejection by my church family would follow me through not only my decade of paganism but for years to come. During this time, my pastor would still occasionally speak with me by phone. It was difficult for me to comprehend how this spiritual solitary confinement was their attempt to bring me back into the fold and, just as confusing, how my pastor cared more about me than I cared about myself, as he often reiterated.

> *"And though it is true that the church must always dissociate itself from sin, it can never have any excuse for keeping any sinner at a distance"*
> —Brennan Manning

On several occasions, I shared conversations with my pastor, during which I, the witch, would quote Scripture in an attempt to ease his concern. For example, "If you have faith as a mustard seed, you will say to this mountain, 'Move from here to there,' and it will move" (Matthew 17:20). I honestly could not understand the fear that many in the church body associated with my presence. It was later explained that the concern lay more with new Christians than those strong in the faith, but even that was hard to fathom. While I may have had my magick, those with a little faith could move mountains!

Admittedly, my conversion to witchcraft must have created shockwaves in my church, because just months before becoming a witch, I was one of their Spirit-filled believers. It would seem insensitive to question their particular concern, but this reaction is not surprising, considering the fact that we are bombarded with "witches infiltrating the church to destroy, kill, and steal" media propaganda, which caused a lot of undue alarm.

One of the main concerns for both Christian parents and church leaders is the infiltration of witchcraft in the church. While we encourage nonbelievers to attend, it is not so with the witch. Now I'm not talking about placing the witch in a leadership role in the church, but rather one simply sitting next to believers on a Sunday morning listening to the gospel message.

I remember Christmas Eve in the Episcopal church I grew up in. We had a yearly attendee who reeked of alcohol yet sang loud enough for the angels in heaven to hear. Granted, he was not the most pleasant in appearance, but his presence during the service was evidence of God's love for the unlovely. The question one needs to ask is this: If a woman smelling like sage; dressed in black garb and boots; and wearing a pentacle around her neck sat next to you on Christmas Eve, would you welcome her with open arms and love her unconditionally?

Inviting a witch to church or having them over for dinner is not in some mysterious way going to convert you into one. In fact, witches are not normally out evangelizing non-seekers into their covens, and more often than not, they may be reluctant in accepting an invitation to church, believing your only motivation is to evangelize them. You may be surprised to learn that it is difficult to find a coven and even harder to become part of one, and, contrary to what we often think, most witches will say their path is not for everyone. Most have been seeking a coven for a while before they discover one.

Regardless of whom we are witnessing to, we should always move in the gifts of the Spirit, discerning spiritual influences and ready to share a word of knowledge if the Holy Spirit imparts one through us. Perhaps what is most important is making sure we are moving in His Spirit and not on our own accord, for our words will come up empty whereas His cut through to the bone and marrow (Hebrews 4:12).

## Fire & Brimstone

One evening I was at the witch shop in a nearby village when a few born-again believers came to picket what they called "the devil's workshop." To this day I remember the conversation with the fire-breathing evangelist who in so many words damned me to eternal hellfire. At the time, I was a practicing witch, but I questioned his right to place judgment upon me.

The scene was dramatic, with their accusations quieting down only when the police arrived. I am sure these well-meaning Christians thought they were doing justice and winning lost souls for Christ, but inside the shop I witnessed an entirely different scenario. Not knowing Jesus personally, patrons saw this "Christian" behavior as an example of the God they served: a God who was judgmental, uncaring, and full of anger, and one who condemned mankind rather than had come in love to save it.

Perhaps these Christians were motivated by a concern for our salvation and thought direct confrontation might best breach the darkness surrounding our understanding. Unfortunately, the result of their enthusiasm was to give Christianity a bad name and drive the Wiccans further from Christ—and possibly many non-Wiccans as well!

## Hunting Down the Devil

*"Do people want what you have, or you can't give it away? ... If people do not see Christ in you, then they don't want what you to have, and if they can't see love, why would they?"*
—Todd White

Several years after my return to Christ, I was attending a church where, perhaps for the first time, I began to fully grasp the amazing grace of God. Pastor Kevin was an anointed teacher who caught the heart of God where grace was concerned. As part of their outreach, the church annually set up a booth at the community street fair, and on this particular day, my spirit became heavy upon hearing this disheartening story.

A young man sporting a T-shirt with a wolf's head within a pentagram walked past the church's booth. While I would have hoped someone would meet him with the love of Jesus, he was pursued like a rabbit being chased by a hound. A sister-in-Christ demanded he tell her the meaning of his shirt (although she already knew the answer), and many at the street fair witnessed her repetitious taunts. The sad thing is that he was the one who smiled and chuckled at her behavior.

One can only wonder how she missed the entire message of grace, and, sadly, this young man drifted off into the crowd. All the while our sister thought she had encountered and intimidated the Enemy, when in actuality another unbeliever drifted further from an understanding of who Jesus really is and the enormous love that lay waiting for him.

During his pagan years, Ron had stopped at a grocery store to pick up a few things, and the clerk recognized the pentagram he was wearing. The hot pursuit began as the mild-mannered store clerk quickly transformed into a Bible-thumping salesman for Jesus and chased him up and down the aisles screaming and shouting. Ron left without buying a thing, including the clerk's dogma.

> We need not be a salesman for Jesus; all we really need to do is to become "like Him."

The problem here is that we need not be a salesman for Jesus; all we really need to do is to become "like Him." Jesus did not hunt down people who were running from Him. On the contrary, people came to Him, from miles around, just to hear Him speak. Yes, Jesus confronted the Enemy who had rendered someone miserable, commanding the demon to come out. But we should also remember that Jesus said He only did what His Father showed Him or told Him to do. Other Bible verses remind us to act in the name of Jesus, which means we are to adopt His ways, not being led by the flesh but moved in agreement with the Father. Unless we ask God what is on His heart as we pray for someone, we will miss the Spirit and see little fruit.

## Off Tract

Mike was a known Wiccan and a special education teacher in his hometown. One day he opened his school desk drawer to find it filled with little comic tracts depicting urban-legend nonsense, such as witch covens putting poison in apples and razors in kids' candy at Halloween. While he had an idea who put the tracts there, the person remained anonymous. This may seem a subtle and nonconfrontational method of evangelism, but he quickly wrote off the message on the tracts because of their erroneous portrayal.

Mike also had a Wiccan friend who received a copy of a novel called *The Crusaders*, which depicted witches doing human sacrifices. The author was off the wall and knew nil of what he was talking about, which once again only discredited his witness.

## The Parable of Mark (Bishop)

There once were four groups of believers ...

In Central Texas was a group that was outraged when Fort Hood allowed Wiccans to meet openly on post. To their credit, these people mellowed out when they realized they now knew who to pray for.

In the Northeast, a gathering of believers has an outreach to the whole community, and especially to witches since there are many in that area.

An affiliate of the Northeast gatherings had their own group, at least until they revoked the pastor's ordination. His downfall? He was too friendly with the witches.

In North Texas is a fellowship that has a simple philosophy: whoever shows up needs to find Jesus. Of course, they also have an outreach to help addicts, witches, alcoholics, etc. Surprisingly, to break all preconceived stereotypes, this group I am referring to is Fundamental Baptist. When someone with an occult history comes to the pastor's attention, he has been known to send them my way.

Which of these four groups do you think is doing more of what Jesus wants?

## Suffer the Witch

Exodus 22:18 says, "Thou shalt not suffer a witch to live." (KJV). Almost every witch has responded to this Scripture with anger and resentment, and unfortunately it is often the first weapon drawn by many Christians. Most witches have heard this verse quoted to them more times than they have heard John 3:16. Personally, I questioned it when compared with another Scripture, "You shall love your neighbor as yourself" (Matthew 22:39), so what do you do if your neighbor is a witch?

Most biblical scholars agree that Exodus 22:18 pertains to many occult activities, such as divination, spell-casting, and any other practices that draw power outside of the one true God; this fits most occult practices, witchcraft being no exception. Yet taken out of context, the verse is one big stumbling block for witches. It seems all too often we do not look at the whole of Scripture from start to finish. God is a holy and jealous God, but He has a gigantic heart for man. In fact, He desired man to be reconciled with Him to the point of giving up His only Son so we could have eternal life with Him, not die in eternal damnation.

*"You shall love your neighbor as yourself" (Matthew 23:39), so what do you do if your neighbor is a witch?*

All too often we take Scripture verses and use them as stones, casting them haphazardly at those we consider evil. If we look at 1 Samuel 15:23, "For rebellion is as the sin of witchcraft, and stubbornness is as iniquity and idolatry," we find something alarming: we find ourselves. We have all rebelled against God and can attest to our own stubbornness. We proudly boast in our obedience but indulge in the flesh from the seduction of the prostitute to the greed in the business suit.

How many times have you wanted to control any aspect of your life and not yielded it to God? In John 8 we read a story about an adulterous woman whom they brought before Jesus, and the crowd suggested she be stoned to death. Jesus answered, "He who is without sin among you, let him throw a stone at her" (v. 7). Are there any among us who is not guilty of rebellion or stubbornness? Verse 9 concludes, "Then those who heard it, being convicted by their conscience, went out one by one, beginning with the oldest even to the last."

## Wiccans Praying in Jesus' Name

One evening I stumbled upon a video on the internet of a street evangelist by the name of Todd White who has a heart for the lost regardless if they be Wiccan, Buddhist, Muslim, or a nonbeliever. He shares a story of three young Wiccan women he walked up to on the streets of Connecticut, and after telling them, "Jesus loves you," he apologized on behalf of the church for the wrong done to them and because this would likely be the first time a Christian initiated a group hug with them.

These girls encountered the love of Jesus through the actions of one of His followers. Todd's story ends with him encouraging two of the Wiccans to lay hands on their friend and pray in the name of Jesus for her healing of a pituitary tumor.

> *"So you need to be the power source of love for them in order for them to enter into the kingdom."*
> —Todd White

Todd offers an explanation and a challenge to us as believers: "They're no different from anybody else. They're just twisted up in their belief system, and a lot of times, with witches, they've been crushed by the church. They've been beat up, so they resort to an alternate source of power that is very limited when they could have had all this. Because they got oppressed and pushed out, they choose another way, and we know Jesus is the way. So you need to be the power source of love for them in order for them to enter the kingdom and to not be afraid to come in."[7]

---

7   "The Witches Testimony – Todd White," *YouTube*, https://www.youtube.com/watch?v=seu-ZSvzuAw.

## Love Your Enemy

"You have heard that it was said, 'You shall love your neighbor and hate your enemy.' But I say to you, love your enemies, bless those who curse, do good to those who hate you, and pray for those who spitefully use you and persecute you" (Matthew 5:43-44). These verses have to be two of the most difficult, because it is rather humbling and goes against our natural fleshly way of thinking, but then our ways are not God's ways. Not only are we to love our enemies, but we are to bless those who curse us. If it is hard to love those who love us, how can we love those who are against us? And not only against us, but against the God we serve?

Why should we love those who worship other gods and practice many abominations toward our God? The answer is simple: because only by loving them will we show the love God has for them. Pagans expect the anger and judgment thrown at them by Christians, and just as I did in the witch shop with the condemning evangelist, they see a furious, cold-hearted, judgmental God. Maybe if we love them, they will experience something beyond hurt and rejection and encounter His unconditional love.

We are the representatives of Jesus to the world. I am convinced that He would draw the lost to Him through us if we could control our "fleshy" reactionary responses to judge the lost or to defend God, and allow the love of Christ to truly live in us. Our God needs no help to defend Himself, nor does He need our help in judging others.

## Reflection & Action

Either by yourself or in a small group, reflect on these questions.

- How do nonbelievers view our overzealous intentions in rescuing souls from the pit of hell?
- What is our commission as the church? What happens when we step out of those bounds?
- What method did Jesus use to draw the multitudes?

How does this compare to the "salesman for Jesus" in this chapter?

- What happens when we rely on urban legends, such as some Christian tracts, to share the gospel?
- Under the section "The Parable of Mark Bishop," answer the question that was asked: Which of these four groups do you think is doing more of what Jesus wants? Explain.
- What Scripture verse is most often quoted to witches? What is the biblical definition for witchcraft?

Check which of the action steps below would be appropriate and realistic for you, or you and others, to take (check all that apply):

- ☐ Role play. Have your study group conduct a scenario with one person playing a Wiccan and another, a Christian witnessing. Use what you have learned to share your faith.

- ☐ Write your own "The Parable of the Pagan" with the moral reflecting God's love for those who truly do not know Him.

- ☐ Volunteer at your church's community outreach, being attentive to any divine opportunities God may send your way to show Jesus' love to someone involved in the occult.

# CHAPTER SIX

## Witchcraft in the Church

My first thought after coming out of witchcraft and stumbling upon a "Christian utopia" seemingly focused on God's love was, *At last!* It was refreshing to see several best-selling Christian authors and some up-and-coming churches adapt a post-modern approach to a "love triumphs" banner. Looking beyond stale, traditional church steeples to find a meaningful spirituality seemed like a breakthrough and a hope that love would finally find its rightful place within believers.

My heart was heavy for the countless pagans I had known whose impression of the God of Christianity was anything but loving. I knew all too well their view of the God portrayed through His followers with hatred and intolerance. During my years as a pagan, I had at least known God in a way that many of these people never had, but even then their portrayal of Jesus grieved me. If only they knew who Jesus *really* was. If only all believers' lives, mine included, reflected the true nature of God and displayed the same love for others He had shown.

After both witnessing and experiencing the hurt, heartbreak, and disillusionment I encountered within the church and/or with Christians, this new move toward

> *Many times it seemed well-intentioned Christians actually dropped cinder blocks onto the path leading toward God, rather than creating a bridge to Him.*

love seemed promising. Many times it seemed well-intentioned Christians actually dropped cinder blocks onto the path leading toward God, rather than creating a bridge leading to Him. Jesus came not for the well but the inflicted, not for the saint but the sinner, and He came not with hostility but with love. I was hopeful after all. Love never fails.

## The Tainted Gospel

I would soon discover that this freestyle, personalized form of Christianity was more aligned with Wicca, as both blended some of the same religious experiences, pagan beliefs, and practices. Not surprisingly, it had become acceptable to be a Christian Muslim, Christian Buddhist, or even a Christian witch because these people considered all people saved without repentance and already part of the kingdom. This all-inclusive theology claimed that there are many ways to reach God, and each path is just one of many. But this is contrary to the Word of God, which says, "Jesus said to him, 'I am the way, the truth, and the life. No one comes to the Father except through Me'" (John 14:6).

If believing all ways lead to God was not bad enough, this movement claimed that sin, hell, and judgment should not be associated with Jesus since God is love. After all, in their minds, what loving God would send one of His creations to hell? Hell was considered a concept, not a literal place. This again aligns with Wiccans' belief that there is no hell, except as a concept in the minds of Christians. Neither group believes in sin, therefore there is no need for a Savior. While one may readily accept this theology from a pagan mindset, a Christian movement eliminating the need for its own Savior is absurd.

> "If Jesus had preached the same message that ministers preach today, He would never have been crucified."
> —Leonard Ravenhill

This movement also did not believe that heaven is a place, or that Jesus will physically return for His bride, the church. Imagine the hopelessness of knowing that this life—

with all its pain, suffering, and disappointments—is all there is. Even the Wiccan belief acknowledges a heaven, called Summerland, where those who have died go to await their next reincarnation. In this case, these emergent views align more with an atheist mindset, with death being the ultimate end and the idea that heaven and hell are just states of mind in the here-and-now and are not literal destinations experienced only in the afterlife.

With this concept there would be no reason for any of the testimonies in this book that attest to the redemptive power of Jesus. According to this movement, each could have continued to practice witchcraft and would still be saved. What has emerged out of this so-called Christian movement is an attempt to merge Christianity with Universalism, the one-world religion that, in itself, is a sign of the end times.

In response to what more realistically could be called the "New Age church," our former witches provide insight into this movement. Taryn shares the deception targeted at the youth: "I believe it is a big deception and a lie from the pit of hell! This kind of mixture will be very attractive to the youth, as it is in Satan's plan to corrupt our children and the future generation. The devil comes as an angel of light, and being the master deceiver, he deceives all that he can and in any which way he can. We need to pray for them that God will lift the veil of evil and enlighten them to the truth!"

The gnostic philosophy set on personal experience over Scripture is examined by Ron: "My opinion of the emergent movement? They reject the authority of the Word of God, they don't believe in hell or judgment. They despise the cross, and discourage rational thinking or clear biblical teaching. They place supernatural experiences above everything else. They also use creative visualization, mind-science, breath prayers/contemplative prayers, walking labyrinths, meditation, and Christian yoga. They are basically the return of Gnosticism. It's pretty much nothing more than the repackaged New Age movement."

## The Serpent in the Sanctuary

Throughout church history, witchcraft has on more than one occasion crept into the church. Sadly, future generations will be no different. Witchcraft comes from rebellion, and the sin of rebellion is a willful refusal to follow God, which results in the willingness to be led by another spirit. It takes only one small element of rebellion, which is easily found in our innately fallen nature, to direct us away from God. Any time we as individuals or the church body disregard God's commands or His Word for our own desires, we are placing ourselves at risk of an alternative spiritual takeover.

The Enemy is subtle, and as the angel of light, he lures us with things that look good or even seem godly. He makes his way into the church by deceiving practices that many times we attribute to a new move of God. Now I'm not condemning the entire prophetic signs and wonders movement. I believe God still speaks through prophets today and exhibits signs and wonders. However, we cannot deny that a counterfeit spirituality lurks in the shadows. Therefore, it is crucial that we hold all things, including our practices, in the light of Scripture. That means we compare the practice or manifestation to make sure it fits with what the Bible says, and not the other way around. The Enemy would have us twist Scripture to justify a non-biblical act.

Within the "Christian utopia," I would soon discover manifestations of uncontrollable laughter and jerking, animalistic and drunken behavior, and daily angelic encounters becoming commonplace in churches. These unusual displays had seeped their way into several denominations, but were especially widespread in the charismatic churches. While many attributed these signs and wonders to the Holy Spirit, others warned of another spirit at work.

In Exodus 7:10, we see Moses and Aaron before Pharaoh, and how Aaron's rod transformed into a serpent. Pharaoh called his sorcerers, who also transformed their own rods into serpents. In the end, Aaron's serpent swallowed the other serpents before becoming a rod again. The point here is that the Enemy's counterfeits can mimic the signs and wonders of God, and if we're not careful, they can lead us down the back alley of destruction. In fact, it is no coincidence that I personally found myself amid these signs and wonders after having come out of the occult.

First John 4 tells us to test the spirits to make sure they are from God, and warns us of the false spirit of the Antichrist. Interestingly, some manifestations mentioned above describe the awakened Kundalini (serpent energy said to be coiled at the base of the spine and the source of the life force)—for instance, jerking, psychic visions, repeated mantras, uncontrollable laughing and/or weeping, and loss of consciousness or a trance-like state. If we hold the same manifestations to the Word of God, we don't find them except in situations of the demon-possessed who, once delivered, returned to a sound mind.

On one occasion, I visited a church where a well-known woman of God shook her head so vigorously that I had to contain myself from laying hands on her to cast out the demonic spirit. Instead I prayed silently, but the next time it happened I followed the lead of the Holy Spirit and verbally told the spirit to flee. Be careful and test all spirits to make sure they align with God's Word. If they do not, you know that the manifestation is from the spirit of the Antichrist.

### Witchcraft in the Pew

Many times when you hear of witchcraft in the pews, you immediately think of witch infiltration. But before you scope out the sanctuary, ready to hurl warfare prayers at a woman wearing a black dress or a young man with his arms full of tattoos, remember that we are talking about something far more sinister—something not as obvious as caution tape around a crime scene.

The Enemy slips occult practices into the church almost unnoticed, or at least in a way that makes them appear innocent and safe. Let's look at some age-old practices the Enemy recirculates in the church to entrap and hinder generation after generation.

## Centering Prayer

One occult practice you may find in the church is contemplative prayer, also known as centering prayer. In this type of prayer, the name of Jesus is used as a mantra despite the biblical reference to avoid repetitious prayer: "And when you pray, do not use vain repetitions as the heathen do. For they think that they will be heard for their many words" (Matthew 6:7).

Eastern meditation practices commonly use the clearing one's mind through mantra chanting, which Wicca also incorporates. One of my earliest witchcraft lessons was to strip my mind of former thoughts, beliefs, and theologies, thus recreating my own through study and meditation. Meditation was one thing I used to enter a trance-like state and communicate with my spirit guide.

Not that meditation itself is unscriptural, for there are numerous biblical references instructing us to meditate on God's Word (Joshua 1:8; Psalm 1:2; Psalm 4:4). The difference with biblical meditation is that it does not empty one's mind and consequently allow sources other than God to fill it through repetitious chants or mantras. Rather, biblical meditation focuses our mind on God, His Word, and His truth. It is through filling the mind with Scripture and reflecting on God's goodness that we are transformed by the renewal of our minds by His Word, as Paul instructs in Romans 12:2.

*The difference with biblical meditation is that it does not empty one's mind and consequently allow sources other than God to fill it.*

Mike shares the similarities between contemplative prayer and New Age meditation: "It starts with a quiet setting, soft music, closing one's eyes, and entering into the presence of God. Often it involves the visualization of being in an 'Eden-like' or heavenly place and coming face-to-face with His presence (whether they "see" God or not). Problem is, it really does not differ from the New Age or Wiccan practice I used for meditation, which included breathing exercises combined with moving my consciousness through the various chakras. While it is true that we find meditation in the Scriptures, the meditation engaged in by the Jews and early Christians can best be summed up in Psalm 119:9-16. Their meditation was upon the Scriptures, the written Word of God."

As with the church today, it didn't take long for the early church to wander from the truth. Biblical meditation became intertwined with Hindu and Buddhist techniques used by the early Christian Desert Fathers (reclusive desert monks), adopting this as a way of achieving union with God. While their initial inspiration may have been Jesus and His teachings, their meditation practices that incorporated Eastern Mysticism or occult practices oozed into the early church.

Mike concludes with this exhortation: "Likewise, for individuals who are fortunate enough never to have had any experience with the occult, it is difficult for them to understand many of these experiences. But like the person who knows the taste of an orange from personal experience, individuals who have been steeped in the occult and its shadows will recognize things occult in nature with crystal clarity. All I can say is that I would caution any person, Christian or otherwise, from engaging in any of these types of practices."

> "But like the person who knows the taste of an orange from personal experience, individuals who have been steeped in the occult and its shadows will recognize things occult in nature with crystal clarity."
> —Mike Morton

## Prayer Labyrinth

A prayer labyrinth is a maze-like path that leads one on a symbolic journey and is used as an aid to contemplative prayer. At different intervals along the path, the spirit traveler finds a mixture of visuals, contemplative words, and art forms to aid in their journey. Some modern-day labyrinths even includes headphones with music, meditations, and instructions for each part of the labyrinth.

Yet the labyrinth's origins didn't begin in medieval cathedrals but rather originated much further back, in caves where the labyrinth was the temple of the Goddess and the path on which dancers performed in her ceremonies. The labyrinth itself is an ancient symbol of wholeness and the journey of life. Walking the labyrinth, one creates sacred space, such as what is created for Wiccan rituals today, and connects with the divine energy along its path.

Shalom shares her experience of walking the labyrinth in a Catholic church while she was a practicing Wiccan: "I am familiar with labyrinth walking, which I gleefully took part when I was practicing Wicca, clad in my black robe and brandishing my athame. No one at the Catholic church where the labyrinth was located seemed to feel that there was anything wrong with it. I don't feel that this practice should be followed by believers, as it is most definitely pagan and exposes one to the potential for opening doors to the demonic."

> *It is amazing to think that after Jesus sets us free and the veil was rent, giving us access into the Holy of Holies, that some still feel the need to revert back to vain prayers, formulas, and repetitions—falling into bondage all over again.*

One need only discern what influence the medieval church was under when it incorporated the symbol of the labyrinth from other pagan cultures into its sanctuaries, or the source behind the reemergence of the labyrinth into some churches today. Putting a Christian label on something does not make it biblical any more than calling someone a Christian makes them a follower of Christ. It is amazing to think that after Jesus sets us free and the veil was rent, giving us access into the Holy of Holies, that some still feel the need to revert back to vain prayers, formulas, and repetitions—falling into bondage all over again.

## Spirit Travel

I once attended a Christian conference and was shocked when an elderly renowned prophet seated alone on a raised platform led the audience through a time of breathing to relax, then encouraged them to let their minds drift before slowly guiding them hypnotically through what he termed "spirit travel"—soaring over mountains and flying through clouds toward heaven in much the same way I had taken shamanic journeys during my pagan years.

As this journey drew to a close, he claimed he was gifted in discerning when demons were present in a church, and joyfully announced that there were none there that day. Little did he know that the demonic influence was not in the crowd, but working through the very expedition he led.

First Thessalonians 5:19–21 tells us, "Do not quench the Spirit. Do not despise prophecies. Test all things; hold fast to what is good." In ancient times, God relayed messages to the prophets through visions and dreams, as He still does today, but we must be able to distinguish the difference between what is from God and what is not. Occult prophesy is obtained through self-induced trance, whereas God reveals His message with no initiative on the prophet's part.

> *In ancient times, God relayed messages to the prophets through visions and dreams, as He still does today, but we must be able to distinguish the difference between what is from God and what is not.*

While Scripture includes numerous instances where the prophet was taken up in a vision to a distant place, it is important to note that the prophet alone went on the journey in his vision; no one went with him. In Ezekiel 8:3 we learn that the prophet was lifted up between earth and heaven, and brought to Jerusalem while the elders of Israel sat before him, and in Daniel 10:7 we see the men who were with Daniel did not see his vision.

As in the case at the conference, prophecy is not a self-induced supernatural joy ride for a group to embark on. All too often we find people who believe they can invoke prophecy on demand, but God does not cater to our demands for signs and wonders. Many today declare themselves to be prophets of God, yet according to Scripture being a prophet was not something one aspired to. Almost every prophet in the Bible did not desire the position and, without exception, their words called people back to God and His standards of holiness. The ministry of the prophet and the prophetic gifts can provide Spirit-empowered revelation; however, we (the church) must use discernment to be sure the prophet is guided by the Holy Spirit and the message is tested to ensure it aligns with God's written Word.

Spirit travel or soul travel, as I experienced at the conference, is a repackaging of astral (mind) projection targeted at the Christian audience. This practice was also encouraged by the Desert Fathers in the early church. Ron, who was well learned in the art of this pagan practice, shares his insight and cautions:

> *"Every reference we see in the Bible about spirit travel was an act initiated by God."*
> —Ron Harnage

Astral projection is an occult practice where one causes their soul to leave their body and wander about in the spirit realm, by means of self-induced trances. I was involved in the occult for over twenty-one years and had heavily practiced altered states of consciousness through these trances. Some ministries are now teaching these same techniques which I once employed, except they are calling it worship, but it is most certainly not by any means worshiping God. Every reference we see in the Bible about spirit travel was an act initiated by God. We don't see anyone employing techniques to arrive at this experience, as it was all done by God and apparently without any warning as to what was about to happen. He did these things to suit His purpose and carry out His will, and we never see it as some form of spiritual entertainment (Ezekiel 37:1; Acts 8:39; 1 Kings 18:12).

In 2 Corinthians 12:2, Paul isn't even sure exactly what happened: "whether in the body I do not know, or whether out of the body I do not know." It is obviously an act of God, and Paul is careful to not get caught up in pride in the experience. Astral projection is very dangerous and leads to bondage to a familiar spirit, and after some time, you will not even do this of your own free will. It is ungodly sorcery, trafficking in the demonic, and it has nothing to do with the physical processes of the mind.

## Christianized Oracles

An oracle can be a person through whom a supposed deity speaks, or hidden (occult) knowledge is revealed by one of many symbolic tools used to facilitate a divine purpose. Many occult oracles exist, and one can use practically anything as one. Below we touch the surface with the most common methods accepted by Christian believers.

### Dream/Destiny Cards

I first heard of Christian dream cards on Facebook, and it didn't take much effort to locate them online. Marketed as colorful laminated cards, they comprise symbols to help people interpret their dreams. I think the most alarming aspect was the title "Christian" placed on their label, and, in my opinion, a more appropriate cover would be the picture of the serpent dangling from a tree with "God didn't say you shouldn't practice divination, did He?" as its quote.

If that is not bad enough, there is actually an entire group of those who claim to be Christians who provide destiny card readings. They proudly promote their seven different card decks used in their readings at numerous secular events, including pagan festivals. In the 1970s, we had The Jesus Deck, a fifty-two-card deck originally designed to educate children about the Bible but turned into a tool of divination for MBS (Mind-Body-Spirit) seekers.

However, as sincere as the dream or destiny interpreter may be, Christianized divination does not differ from its counterfeit.

Do not get me wrong, dream interpretation is found in numerous stories in the Bible where prophets both received dreams and the insight to interpret them. However, Daniel did not pull from a dream deck any more than Joseph whipped out his dream symbology book to aid in his interpretation.

> *Daniel did not pull from a dream deck any more than Joseph whipped out his dream symbology book to aid in his interpretation.*

During my Wiccan years, I used to keep a dream journal by my bed, and upon awakening I would record my dream and any specific thoughts or symbols. We usually went by our own intuition for the symbolic meaning of our dream, but at times we would resort to a dream book as a guide. Dreams and their interpretation were often a topic we engaged in between coven members or like-minded friends. However, the fascination with the meaning of dreams is not confined to pagans; it is held by the general population. How many times have you been in line at the grocery store or at work and overheard someone talking about the dream they had the night before? While I believe God still speaks through dreams today, and we all have had dreams that thwart our understanding, it is the method used to seek the interpretation where the Enemy leads us astray.

Mike sums it up this way: "When Pharaoh couldn't interpret his dreams and his soothsayers failed, it was Joseph, the man of God who could do so. When Nebuchadnezzar had a dream and couldn't remember it, and his soothsayers couldn't do it, he gave the order for all the soothsayers and wise men to be slain. But God gave Daniel the dream and interpretation, and in Daniel 2:28 he gives the glory to God: 'There is a God in heaven who reveals secrets.'"

However, even in the (generic) Christian realm there are some who try to penetrate the church and world with ungodly dream-interpretation practices that are clearly New Age. I believe this is Satan's attempt to deceive us in these last days, when God promises that He will pour out His Spirit on all flesh, that the young men and women will dream dreams, and the old men and women will have visions (Joel 2:28).

## Angel Cards

Similar to dream cards are angel cards, which often give the illusion of being biblical since angels are referenced in Scripture as messengers of God, but just because these cards come packaged with angelic images, does not make their answers from God. Mike gives his insight on angel cards: "These are like tarot cards and are considered 'oracles.' That is, they are used for divination. Too many Christians hear the word *angel* and think it automatically is Christian (or possibly Jewish) in nature. This couldn't be further from the truth. They forget that Satan is a fallen angel—the "chosen cherubim" (Isaiah 14 and Ezekiel 28 describe his origins and fall) and that angels can also be found throughout New Age and the occult. I believe that invoking these spirits is akin to wrapping your soul in chains and falling under their control instead of you controlling them! I consider these cards (and any other oracle cards or tarot cards) deadly in your spiritual walk."

My pastor once said, "The errant use of these cards should not, however, render angels as unwelcome visitors since they are ministering spirits that God uses to bring messages or provide protection. However, angelic beings are not to be worshiped or consulted, and we should be watchful lest we are fooled into being led away from God by demons appearing as angels."

## Tattoo Interpretation

An even more unorthodox form of divination is tattoo interpretation, which is being done by Christians who lay claim to hidden prophetic and symbolic messages in tattoos and piercings. Tattoos and piercings are very much a part of the current generation, and since many have also experienced disillusionment with Christianity, they are susceptible to this type of divination.

The tattoo interpreter uses the same basic concept as any other form of divination to give a reading, this time on the individual's tattoo or piercing. If you have not figured it out by now, divination by any name or form is strictly divination. Ron confirms, "I guess there's always some new trendy thing going on, such as the tattoo and piercing interpretation, but you can do divination with anything, really."

> *Whatever method of divination is used, the desire to gain forbidden knowledge has its roots in the garden where the serpent first tempted Eve to be like God and know good and evil.*

Whatever method of divination is used, the desire to gain forbidden knowledge has its roots in the garden where the serpent first tempted Eve to be like God and know good and evil. It was the downfall of man in the beginning and continues to be so today. Attempting to gain knowledge through divination is our own act of rebellion and is an open invitation for demonic influences to gain access in our lives. The Enemy uses rebellion to blind our spiritual eyesight and thus prevent us from seeing the truth or discerning the spiritual influence we have unknowingly become subjected to.

## Christian Yoga

Is Christian Yoga Too Much of a Stretch?

Christians often see yoga simply as beneficial exercise. We are each responsible for taking care of our body, especially considering it is the temple of the Holy Spirit (see 1 Corinthians 6:1–30), so why not incorporate it into our daily lives? Exercise is good not only for our bodies, but our minds as well. We should strive to maintain a healthy weight and keep our bodies fit. So what could be wrong with a low-impact exercise regimen? Furthermore, two of the fruits of the Spirit are peace and self-control. Since yoga appears to share the common goals of achieving peace, self-discipline, and self-awareness, this would seem to be the perfect union of mind and body. After all, some churches encourage and even hold yoga classes under their steeples.

Before we are too quick to assume the Lotus position, let's take a deeper look at this Hindu practice. According to *Yogapedia*, yoga comes from the Sanskrit word *yug*, which means unite. The next question we must ask is, "To unite with what?" Is it simply a union of body and mind? Reading further in our definition, we discover the union is referring to "uniting individual consciousness (our individual experience of reality) with a Divine consciousness (the essence of truth as perceived when we quiet our five senses)."[8] Our next question must be, "What is this Divine consciousness we are marrying?"

For insight into the spiritual roots of yoga, we reference Pastor Mike Shreve, who taught Kundalini yoga at four Florida universities before becoming a Christian.

"According to yogic lore, there are seven chakras, or spiritual energy centers, in the body. The first five are located along the spine. The sixth is the 'third eye' and the seventh is the crown chakra, located at the top of the head. Adherents believe that something called 'the kundalini' (the latent 'serpent power' supposedly coiled at the base of the spine) rises up through the chakras, especially during deep meditation. This 'awakening of the kundalini' is considered essential in bringing a person to 'God-consciousness.' It is also important to note that each chakra is associated with a certain Hindu deity. These deities are all mythical beings, full of human-like frailties and faults."[9]

So we find the Divine consciousness that yoga practitioners are uniting with are Hindu deities. Uniting one's consciousness with Hindu gods is idolatry, and in direct opposition with God. Mike also explains that yoga practitioners are taught how to "exit their body through the chakras and experience higher spiritual realms." As mentioned earlier in this chapter regarding spirit travel, these practices are a gateway to the occult. Mike shares, "I was actually overtaken by demonic beings that granted me false experiences of the supernatural world. Upon receiving Jesus as

---

8  Jennie Lee, "What Is The True Meaning Of Yoga?" Yogapedia, January 12, 2017, https://www.yogapedia.com/what-is-the-true-meaning-of-yoga/2/9038.
9  Mike Shreve, "Five Main Reasons Why I No Longer Practice Hatha Yoga," Whollyfit.com, http://www.wholyfit.com/wp-content/uploads/2012/01/mikeShreve.pdf.

Lord of my life, I was delivered from these spirits."

"But," you may say, "I just do yoga for the stretching, flexibility, and exercise, and omit any spiritual connection." But can you truly separate the two? One must remember that they name these practices after the gods of Hinduism, and when you hold these postures, it's meant to invoke the nature, properties, and attributes of other gods. Yoga, even Hatha yoga practiced in the Western world as flexibility exercises and said to be without spiritual influence, utilizes poses that by design were created with the intent to open oneself to power—power that we as Christians know is demonic in nature. Therefore, there is no separating the two, as they are intrinsically connected.

> *"I was quite surprised, though not dismayed when my guru taught us that yoga was really witchcraft."*
> — Mike Shreve.

In fact, if you look closely, you'll begin to see a strong similarity between yoga and witchcraft. *Witchcraft?* Yes, that's right. Let's refer back to Mike Shreve. "I was quite surprised, though not dismayed initially because I was so caught up in it, when my guru taught us that yoga was really witchcraft."[10] Even if you omit blending your consciousness with Hindu deities and avoid an out-of-body experience or reciting a mantra, the poses themselves are an open-door invitation to an alternative spirituality that counters the very Word of God.

Perhaps you've taken a class or two and avoided any spiritual implications. Does that mean you play on train tracks because you've avoided being struck? It's a spiritual train wreck waiting to happen. May we not sacrifice our soul on the altar of compromise. Some physical alternatives to yoga are low-impact aerobics, isometrics, walking, and jogging. Walking and jogging are also great opportunities to get outdoors and spend time praying, hearing from God, speaking to Him, and thanking Him for His

---

10  "Delivered from Witchcraft with Mike Shreve," Charisma Podcast Network, https://www.charismapodcastnetwork.com/show/charismanews/b0f9f773091b-42b6a8cfec740af867c4.

wonderful creation.

Philippians 4:6–7 says, "Do not be anxious about anything, but in every situation, by prayer and petition, with thanksgiving, present your requests to God. And the peace of God, which transcends all understanding, will guard your hearts and your minds in Christ Jesus."

## Invasion of the Grave Suckers

This subheading sounds like a science-fiction thriller, but it's not. Rather, it is a practice taking place in some prominent churches today. What is it? In short, an attempt to extract the anointing from the empowered departed, kind of like using an E-ZPass in the fast lane to your chosen ministry. Those who take part in this cryptic practice attempt to validate it by comparing it to the passing of a mantle, such as when Elijah passed his mantle of authority to Elisha.

However, Elijah's mantle was passed when the prophet was taken up into heaven, not from his grave. And both Elijah and Elisha participated in the mantle passing; it did not happen hundreds of years after Elijah had passed. This mantle-grabbing practice was taken further into the grave with Elisha's bones. Second Kings 13:21 tells of how a man being buried was cast down into Elisha's sepulcher, and after touching Elisha's bones he was revived. Now, Elisha's mantle did not fall down on him from heaven, nor did he take up Elisha's ministry; rather, he was brought back to life. Yet somehow today, we have believers flocking to graveyards, hugging tombstones and soaking on plots hoping to get the anointing right out of them dry bones.

When this subject was brought to the attention of Shalom, her reaction was, "Oh my, this is a subject that points up so well how paganism has infested the church and is corrupting Christianity!" She digs in to what she believes to be the root cause of this ghoulish practice: "As anyone who has studied demonology will understand, demons are *very* legalistic! Every time we do not walk in accord with God's instructions, we give legal ground to the demonic realm to influence our lives. This is as natural a consequence as jumping off a ten-story building and splatting onto the ground, for not paying attention and respecting the law of gravity. All a demon wants is a toe-hold because they are quite adept at using a small entry to carve a much larger one."

Mike provides insight on the ways the demonic enter in through this practice: "Many in the occult will attempt to draw energies from the graves of the dead. For example, the tomb of Mary Leveau, the most famous (or infamous) Voodoo priestess and practitioner in New Orleans' history, is a mecca for many who wish to utilize the spirits of Voodoo, and they will leave offerings and do rituals at her tomb to acquire the power that she had. There is nothing in Scripture that can be used to support such a bizarre practice. Their actions are occult in nature, and heretical."

> *"Simon (once a sorcerer), after his salvation, thought to purchase the power of God, and Peter rebuked him harshly for it (Acts 8:9–24). If you want the bottom line, it is this: Why should a child of God live on stolen leftovers?"*
> —Mark Bishop

This graveside coveting ritual's focus is to steal an anointing, but the fact remains that we cannot beg, steal, or borrow a mantle bestowed upon another by God. Mark concurs, "Not only does this beg the question of why would God's children be doing this, but Simon (once a sorcerer), after his salvation, thought to purchase the power of God, and Peter rebuked him harshly for it (Acts 8:9–24). If you want the bottom line, it is this: Why should a child of God live on stolen leftovers?"

I contacted one church that has been noted to engage in this practice and was told they knew of some of their congregation's participation but did not want to discourage the "fire" within these believers. So, believing it was not dangerous, they did not condemn the practice. April addresses this supposedly innocent act: "All I can say is that what they are doing is spiritually dangerous, not just because of any power exchange but because of the sin of pride. In thinking they can have and wield personal power without God, they fall back into the original sin in the garden of Eden and the biggest sin in pagan practices."

Victoria offers a heartfelt plea: "Grave sucking not only makes us believers look like complete lunatics, because there is not a single Scripture to support this nonsense, and God's divine nature is also in jeopardy under this insanity. Furthermore, why would God tell His followers to lie down on an unclean gravesite to receive a lost portion of the Holy Spirit? In Numbers 12:16 we are instructed to avoid even touching a grave, yet believers go beyond touching and sprawl their entire bodies over its length."

Mike brings the point to rest: "If it were possible for some 'energy' to transfer from the dead body to a living person, we cannot be sure at all that it would be a godly energy. This sounds dangerously close not just to necromancy (communication or receiving anything from the dead) but to modern Voodoo practitioners who attempt to draw the 'mantle' of their greatest practitioner."

Most Wiccans do not practice this type of necromancy, as they would consider it black magick, which they highly discourage. With that said, it is baffling to learn that some Christians are dabbling in dark arts that most witches dare not tread.

## Conclusion

The Enemy uses the same tricks wrapped in a different package based on the spiritual needs of that generation. For instance, in 1970 it was The Jesus Deck, and in the twentieth century dream cards and destiny cards infiltrated the body of Christ. All of these are forms of divination, an occult practice forbidden by God. Yet because they appear light and are labeled "Christian," many believers all too readily endorse them as acceptable.

The Enemy is slick, deceiving the church into seeking answers in cards or anything other than God, and in doing so, he paralyzes the church by a spirit of deception. His next maneuver is to get us to believe that using methods that the world seeks will reach those who never would have come to any church event on their own.

During my Wiccan years, I can honestly say coming across Christian dream cards or the use of spirit travel would not have opened my mind to Christ. In fact, it likely would have had the reverse effect and I would have considered it yet another hypocrisy giving me more reason to reject any part of Christianity. Or as in Shalom's experience, the pagan practice of walking the labyrinth in a cathedral would in no way lead her to the cross and the love of Jesus.

I remember the words spoken to me in the still of the night: "Who do you say I am?" And I recall my pastor confirming it was the voice of Jesus seeking to rescue me as I stood on a spiritual cliff. It was ultimately Jesus. His love set me free, not a love with no absolutes that says "anything goes," but a furious love that stopped at nothing to bring restoration and healing to my wandering soul.

## Reflection & Action

Either by yourself or in a small group, reflect on these questions.

- What are some ways the Enemy deceives the church?
- How did the Enemy attempt to twist the biblical teaching of heaven and hell?
- What is contemplative prayer and how does it compare to New Age teaching?
- True or false: Christian dream cards and angel cards must be acceptable since they carry a Christian label? Explain.
- Where does the labyrinth originate? Should this practice be incorporated in the church?
- What is divination? What do we open ourselves up to when we engage in its practice?

Check which of the action steps below would be appropriate and realistic for you, or you and others, to take (check all that apply):

- ☐ Have your study group research dream interpretations in the Bible. Discuss the difference between the revelation received from God through dreams and the interpretation by man.
- ☐ Research and determine what divination is according to the Bible. Discuss why God prohibits this practice, and explain the difference between it and casting lots as the disciples did.
- ☐ Write a short essay explaining what you would say to a Christian friend who practiced Christian yoga?

# FROM THE CRAFT TO CHRIST

# CHAPTER SEVEN

## Witnessing to the Witch

God's heart is for all men not to perish but be restored to relationship with Him. He desires that none would be lost—even the witch next door, your daughter's Wiccan friend, and the pagan who lives down the street.

The fall of mankind played out in the garden of Eden when the crafty serpent planted the seed of doubt in Eve's mind: "Did God say you must not eat from any tree in the garden?" (see Genesis 3:1–6). The father of lies perverted the truth by bending what God said and portraying God as the oppressor. He uses the same tactic today, twisting the Word of God in attempt to have us believe that witches cannot come back to God or, at the least, Christians should avoid them at all cost. This hidden agenda is the Enemy's attempt to take our focus away from God's desire of restoration of those He loves. The sin of witchcraft is what we should avoid, not those entangled in its practices.

If the Enemy cannot convince you to avoid witnessing to witches, his next attempt will be to instill fear within you. Fear is paralyzing, as it prevents one from freely moving in the Holy Spirit. This can cause you to fall prey to concerns for your own safety or well-being, rather than put your trust in God. My taking a seat in church while still a practicing witch caused an evacuation of the entire row!

Second Timothy 1:7 tells us, "For God has not given us a spirit of fear, but of power and of love and of a sound mind." While it takes a certain amount of courage to witness to a witch, you will find it is not as difficult as you might think. Most witches at least understand the spiritual realm, and just like you and I, were created by God with a spiritual need only He can fill. Most are content with the path they have chosen and do not want you to witness to them at all.

So then, how do you reveal the love of God to a witch? Move in the Spirit, not in the flesh. How many times have our best intentions driven a wedge between someone and God? Unlike God, we only see in part and cannot know what experiences have occurred in an individual's life. In our limited understanding, we are unaware of their true spiritual state and how we can best minister to them at that moment.

Sadly, we often become hindrances to the moving of the Holy Spirit rather than vessels being used by God. I remember many frustrating conversations with well-meaning Christians whose intentions were good but whose attempts were fruitless because they were led by their own flesh and understanding. That same example can be found in every other testimony: meaningful attempts that left negative results.

> "For the hearts of this people have grown dull. Their ears are hard of hearing, and their eyes they have closed, lest they should see with their eyes and hear with their ears, lest they should understand with their hearts and turn, so that I should heal them."
> —Matthew 13:15

This is one reason it is so important to have the heart and mind of our heavenly Father—so we can have a compassionate love for those involved in the occult (Matthew 13:15). Using 1 Corinthians 14 as a barometer, we gain an understanding of agape love crucial for success in reaching the wounded and alienated heart. More important than the words we say is the gospel of love we live.

## Exhibit the Fruit of the Spirit

Use the gifts of the Holy Spirit to minister and exhibit the true nature of God. The fruits of the Spirit are love, joy, peace, long-suffering, kindness, goodness, faithfulness, gentleness, and self-control (Galatians 5:22–23). Recognize that your reactions even when you least expect it are being observed. My friend Bo was witness to my journey while I was in the Craft and explains,

It should come as no surprise that many times the Enemy is looking to disrupt the communication between both you and the witch, and this may come in various forms ranging from just a simple misunderstanding with no known origin, to an outright attack on our God, belief, and faith. That is why it is so important to be prayed up and moving in the right gifting so you do not fall into the temptation of responding in the flesh. Anger, hostility, confusion, pride, self-righteousness, impatience, and even sarcasm are just a few of the traits the Enemy wants you to display so the conversation will be derailed, if not stopped completely. Read Galatians 5:22–23 and engrave it not just on your mind and soul but on your spirit, for what good is it to win the argument but lose the war.

Many preach the Word without living it and then cannot comprehend why nonbelievers do not jump at the chance to be just like them. Be real. Would your lifestyle be an example of Jesus', thus causing others to thirst after it? If not, why not? If we live our lives as Jesus did, we will naturally draw those around us because the love of God flows through us.

> *"When people look at the church and see only impostors, they conclude that Jesus is an impostor. But when they see followers of Jesus who are real, they see a Jesus who is real."* — Mike Yaconelli

## Know Who You're Ministering To

Your conversation with a Satanist should differ from your conversation with a witch. Having basic knowledge of the beliefs of the person you are witnessing to will go a long way. For instance, while you may intend to save their soul from hell, the Satanist may look forward to it and the witch will not believe it exists.

Many times Christians, knowing I was a witch, would assume I was involved in many of the stereotypes associated with the Craft, when that could not have been further from the truth. It took away the importance of what was being said, and discredited what was being shared with me no matter the topic at hand. Before you attempt to tell others what they are involved in, make sure you know the truth. If you do not have knowledge of a particular belief, it is far better to simply say so.

Witches are on a spiritual journey much like you, only they believe there are many ways leading to the same destiny. Chances are you are not the first person to impose "the one and only way" to them. I can tell you, it will not readily be accepted and will likely be viewed as imposing your belief on theirs. Respecting their differences may seem hard to fathom, but ultimately it will win their respect and, in time, allow the love of God to shine through you.

## Prayer, Praise, and Intercession

*As Christians, we know that prayer is a powerful weapon, but remember that we are not fighting flesh and blood but rather with spiritual wickedness in high places, so do not wield your spiritual sword on physical targets.*

As Christians, we know that prayer is a powerful weapon, but remember that we are not fighting flesh and blood but rather spiritual wickedness in high places, so do not wield your spiritual sword on physical targets. Many times we get frustrated when the person we are sharing with either does not seem to get what we are trying to say or is outright hostile toward it. Usually the most defensive and argumentative person has already heard the gospel and their heart has already been pricked by it, which is the Holy Spirit at work.

We somehow get the impression that suiting ourselves in the armor of God is for the offense so we can beat them into the kingdom, or at least drag them there kicking and screaming. Jesus gave us the Great Commission, which instructs us to go and tell; it does not say we have to convince them, which releases us from the heavy burden we load upon ourselves. We cannot save even one soul—not even our own—so release the person and trust them to the Holy Spirit.

With that said, I cannot only express the importance of prayer. Equally essential is praise, which affects the spiritual environment and breaks down spiritual barriers. In 2 Chronicles 5:13–15 we see that God dwells in the praises of His people, therefore when we praise, His presence falls upon us and pushes the darkness away, allowing God to reveal His truth and love. Joshua 6:30 tells us how the walls of Jericho fell with the shout of praise as God brought victory to His people.

My wall of spiritual darkness crumbled during praise and worship. I must admit, I was completely caught off guard and totally overcome by His presence. At the time I was a witch and thought I would prove that the things of God could not move me, but He had another plan. Psalm 149:6 declares, "Let the high praises of God be in their mouth, and a two-edged sword [the Word of God] in their hand."

### Intercession

For the ones God has called to intercede on behalf of those involved in any aspect of the occult, it is crucial to pray against all occult involvement and demonic influence, and for healing of a broken heart, before entering intercession that might include an element of spiritual warfare. Inter-

"To open their eyes, in order to turn them from darkness to light, and from the power of Satan to God, that they may receive forgiveness of sins and an inheritance among those who are sanctified by faith in Me." —Acts 26:18

cession calls for an intimate relationship with Jesus and to be spiritually suited (see Ephesians 6:10–20).

A soul blinded by a veil of deception cannot see God's truth, as the Enemy covers their spiritual eyes and no amount of coercing can convince them to believe. Approaching them at this point only leads to frustration on our part and can cause them to withdraw further from God. Before they can consciously decide, we must pray to lift the deception that clouds their thoughts and blinds their eyes.

Our approach therefore would be in response to the admonition in Zechariah 4:6, which tells us that anything we want to see happen to help another come closer to God—anything we might want to do to build God's kingdom—should first start in the spiritual realm: "'Not by might nor by power, but by my Spirit,' says the LORD." With that said, we pray for the veil of deception to be lifted so that the person we are praying for can see God's truth and freely make a conscious decision to receive the gospel message. We cannot expect someone to understand their need for forgiveness if they do not recognize their sin.

As we pray, it releases God's power, breaking through any resistance and allowing the light of Jesus to pierce through. Jesus instructed believers to pray in the Spirit in Mark 16:17, "In My name they will cast out demons; they will speak with new tongues," for in doing so, we pray in unction with the Holy Spirit for the will of God. We should not lose heart in praying. Depending on occult involvement, it can take time before the veil lifts, and until that time much of our prayer will be in the confines of our prayer closet. Colossians 4:2–6 tells us to continue earnestly in prayer, for this clears the way for eyes to see and ears to hear.

Whether the witch agrees or acknowledges it, there are spiritual entities that may interfere with their eyes being opened to the way, the truth, and the life. This is where you may experience resistance and your intercession may cross over to spiritual warfare. If we look at Jesus' approach in casting out demons, we find that he tended to the individual's physical needs before he took authority over them. We read in Luke 8:35, "Then they went out to see what had happened, and came to Jesus, and found the man from whom the demons had left, sitting at the feet of Jesus, clothed and in his right mind. And they were afraid." Once the man had the legion of demons cast out of him, he could be in his right mind, and could receive truth and be in a relationship with Jesus.

Likewise, I can attest that during my witchcraft years, my mind had become void to the things of God and I could not see His truth. I was deceived, though at the time I believed I was enlightened and thought my mind was free. The truth had been perverted and my unbelief left me vulnerable. Once the veil of deception lifted, I could see truth. I prayed and asked for forgiveness for my wandering heart and ungodly ways. That moment God restored my relationship with Him through the precious blood of Jesus.

A note on spiritual warfare as my pastor once taught: A more accurate translation of the Greek in Matthew 18:18 would read, "Whatever is bound in heaven can be bound on earth, and whatever is loosed in heaven can be loosed on earth." So if we want to be effective in binding demons, we need to know what has already been bound in heaven, and such knowledge is acquired through discernment. That is one reason that some attempt to take authority over a demon and miss, making it appear there is no power in Jesus' name when in fact Jesus has never and will never be defeated by the Enemy.

> *Over the years you have probably heard of various ways to reach those for the kingdom of God, but I can testify that love is the answer.*

## An Illustration of His Love

Church discipline, rejection, and brimstone preaching did not get me any closer to God, but His love was something I could not resist. Over the years you have probably heard of various ways to reach those for the kingdom of God, but I can testify that love is the answer. Witches are usually learned in their own and other beliefs, and they are likely prepared for an argument before you have even engaged in it, but they are not expecting you to simply love them. You are the living testament of Jesus' unconditional love, and by being filled with His love you have a wonderful opportunity to resolve the misconceptions they have about God. Let your life be an illustration of His love. It is not in the words you say, but in your actions, that God's love is revealed.

### Can I Get A Witness?

One challenge my good friend Bo had was finding a legitimate ex-witch to put me in touch with. I had agreed to speak only with someone who was once involved, but I did not want to waste my time with a wannabe whose claim to witchery came from reading a book or watching *Charmed*.

It amazed me when he found a legitimate ex-witch who ran a ministry to aid others in finding their way out of the Craft. Talking with someone who could relate to my spiritual mindset and the rejection I experienced within my church was so helpful. She shared her own experience without insisting I follow suit and became a beacon of light in my darkness.

Miracle overnight conversions are possible but not likely, and more often than not, coming out of the Craft is a process that takes time and patience. I am blessed to have my mentor Lupe's testimony as part of this book, and pray it will impact others in much the same way it did me.

If you do not know a former witch who can assist you in reaching the witch you are ministering to, contact us at www.ex-witch.com or reach out to us through Facebook.

### Respect the One Who Chooses Not to Follow

This has to be the most challenging because we all want our friend or loved one to receive the same saving grace we have, but what if they are not interested? Difficult as it may seem, we have to respect their choice and realize that God has given each of us free will. If God does not force His will on us, what right do we have to force ours on others? That does not mean we lose hope that the individual will ever receive salvation; on the contrary, we should continue to pray as led by God's Holy Spirit, trusting a seed of love was planted and will nourish and grow over time.

Every personal testimony in this book represents an individual who, on their journey, turned away the offer of salvation only to accept and embrace it at a later time in their spiritual walk. Do not be a hound dog chasing after a friend or loved one who has showed they are not interested in your spirituality. Leave that to the "Hound of Heaven" (English poet Francis Thompson wrote a popular poem that depicts God as the Hound of Heaven in His relationship with man).

Before engaging in spiritual warfare, ask God to give you discernment about any demonic foe that is trying to hold fast and say, "In the name of Jesus, I bind that demon of _____ affecting my friend." Then you may have the chance to talk to them unhindered by the Enemy.

## Reflection & Action

Either by yourself or in a small group, reflect on these questions.

- Why is it important to have the heart and mind of our heavenly Father when witnessing to a witch?
- Are the fruits you are exhibiting genuine enough to cause others to thirst after them? If not, why not?
- How can you win the respect of a witch so the love of God will be revealed through/in you?
- How can praise and prayer change the spiritual environment? What first must be broken for darkness to be pierced and for truth revealed?
- What great opportunity do you have that can resolve the misconceptions pagans have about God?

- What do you do if the person you have been trying to reach is not interested in converting from paganism to Christianity?

Check which of the action steps below would be appropriate and realistic for you, or you and others, to take (check all that apply):

- ☐ In chapter 2 you selected and committed to pray for someone who is a pagan or a witch. Pray for the Holy Spirit's guidance in approaching them with a smile, starting a conversation (look for common ground), apologizing for the sins of the church, and establishing an open dialogue and friendship based on mutual interest, not spiritual differences.

- ☐ Invite your study group (make sure they exhibit the love and grace shared in these chapters) and your pagan or witch friend on a nature hike or beach outing, or even to a backyard barbecue. Let your deeds show the love of Christ at work in your life, and proclaim the message of the gospel.

- ☐ At the Holy Spirit's leading, invite your Wiccan friend to church or perhaps to a Christian concert. Be open to answering questions, and share as the Spirit leads. Remember, salvation comes from the Lord, not through a man or woman, so let God be God and be content with being a friend. Sit back and watch what God does.

# PART II

*New Creations in Christ ...*

*Former Witch Testimonies*

# FROM THE CRAFT TO CHRIST

# Chapter Eight

## Mike Morton

*Mike was driven for over 20 years pursuing the path of witchcraft; he became an initiated witch and was elevated to the Third Degree in the Black Forest Clan before beginning his own Wiccan study group. Eventually he became the clan head over two covens in Massachusetts, until he was confronted by the Apostle Paul on Mars Hill.*

My name is Michael. I am in my late 50s at the time I'm writing this, and until about four years ago I had spent nearly 20 years heavily involved in witchcraft. Where did it all begin? I was born and raised Roman Catholic and attended parochial schools through high school. However, while I had been baptized, and made my first confession and first communion, I never was confirmed. My mother was angry because I had blown off the classes that the church conducted to prepare for confirmation. Still, I received a strong Catholic indoctrination through the nuns who taught the schools I attended. The schools had masses that we attended as a student body. While in my teens, often we were given writing assignments including short stories and reports. Many of mine had witchcraft as a main theme. In retrospect, it is interesting that none of the nuns who were my teachers ever suggested that witchcraft or magick were inappropriate.

### The Great Temptation

I remember reading books on mythology and my Aunt Betty regularly shared her books on the supernatural with my parents. I remember reading copies of FATE magazine and pouring over the articles and stories, wishing I could send away for instructions on spells and magick in the classified ads. As a teen I was able to find a few books on witchcraft, but most of them were third-hand accounts of someone who knew someone who knew someone who had been a witch and the other books were nothing more than the stuff that the horoscope magazines in the checkout counters would offer. My aunt gave me a book that included all kinds of occult information and I tried lots of spells. I would go to the bookstores in Harvard Square and go through their occult sections trying to memorize what I could because I didn't have the money to buy them. But, being a teen I lacked a lot of discipline and concentration necessary to make spells work. Some friends may have picked up I was a "dabbler" as my high school yearbook from 1972 had this comment under my picture, "practices witchcraft?"

## Higher Education

I went to college at a communications school in Boston and it was there that I first really heard the gospel of Jesus Christ and committed my life to Him. I forsook my interest in witchcraft and followed Jesus. I moved for about nine months into a Christian community but my tenure there was limited as I seldom got up for their morning prayer sessions. Yet, despite it all, I was growing. The same organization that provided these communities met regularly, sometimes at homes, sometimes at the YMCA, and sometimes at one college in Boston, and I would attend. They were quite original in reaching the youth as they would take popular songs that were on the radio and rewrite the lyrics to Christian themes. After the singing there was a time of teaching and then time for anyone who wanted to share or testify.

In the mid-1970s, after graduating from college with a degree in broadcasting and journalism, I worked in a variety of jobs and lived at home... which worked out well. I saw a special on public broadcasting about Pentecostal churches that made sense. I'd read the Book of Acts and felt that Jesus was the same now... as He was back then. Hebrews 13:8 says, "Jesus Christ is the same yesterday, today, and forever." They mentioned the Assemblies of God and there was one not too far away from my house so I occasionally attended.

## The Un-restorable Breech

In 1975 I made one of the biggest mistakes in my life... I got married. There was no love; nothing solid but we married because everyone else was. Now, almost forty years later I look back and ask, "What was I thinking?" The marriage was painful and both of us were guilty of a lack of love. I had joined the United States Air Force in 1978. My wife accompanied me, but always had difficulties with my assignments. I was assigned to the high desert in California which was actually quite beautiful and she hated it... I was later assigned to the gulf coast of Florida which was equally, if not more beautiful, and she hated that too.

In 1980, my wife went to visit her family back in California and, at the suggestion of her parents who didn't care for me; she aborted our child. This act of distrust was the breech that could never be restored. She didn't want to be a mother and if I would have known this beforehand, I'd never have gotten married. That pretty much shipwrecked any hope for reconciliation. We ended up staying together in misery for a few years, and then in 1983 my oldest daughter Jess was born. The hostility between us remained, but for her sake, we remained together.

Spiritually I had kept plugging along all these years. I tried to do what the Bible taught... but I also kept feeling like I was getting nowhere in my marriage. I preferred smaller churches, so I attended a Calvary Chapel in California as well as the base chapel and an International Foursquare Gospel (Pentecostal) Church. She attended but was never pleased with any of them.

## Tour of Duty

In 1985 I was assigned my first tour of duty to Greenland at Sondrestrom Air Base, about one hundred miles above the Arctic Circle and it was during this time that I had considered the possibility that the Lord might send me back one day to share the gospel, not just with the military, but also with the general population. After my tour of duty I returned to Florida and my wife had found a large church but I was never comfortable there. I found a local Christian FM radio station and served there for a couple years as the Friday night and holiday overnight announcer and it was there that someone introduced me to a pastor of the local Pentecostal Church of God assembly. We started attending and things were going fine. One day, the pastor asked me to seriously pray about and consider becoming a minister in that denomination. After some prayer, I agreed and applied to the Florida council. I went with the pastor to their offices in Tampa and was given my certificate as an Exhorter (basically a minister in training). I labored for a year with exhaustive Bible study materials and reading the Bible through in its entirety. After a year, I received my license and began to serve as the associate pastor at the Cornerstone Pentecostal Church of God.

In 1989 it all fell apart or so it seemed. I had requested a second tour of duty in Greenland as I wanted to bring the gospel there and do some evangelism. Initially, I had orders back to Sondrestrom, but that got changed and suddenly I found myself at Thule Air Base which is about as remote as you can get... about eight hundred miles from the North Pole. The chapel community was awesome, but living in such a remote location was unbearably hard and it was about this time we decided to divorce which became a huge dilemma. Unlike many denominations, the Pentecostal Church of God has a strict policy that if someone is divorced, except for reasons of spousal infidelity, then they lose their license to minister. And so, everything seemed to implode all at once in one glorious fireball. My assignment was difficult, my marriage was dead and divorce was on the horizon. If I had been smart, I would have drawn closer to the Lord, but I wasn't. Instead, I began to blame God, venting such thoughts as, "You sent me to this crap hole instead of to Sondrestrom!", "You let me get married to her!", and, "You let her abort our child!", and the more I allowed myself to be angry at God... the more I started to hate Him. I returned to the United States and went through with the divorce. I ended up leaving the Air Force because they stationed me in California and my daughter was in Massachusetts and I couldn't deal with being a "long distance daddy" and try as I might, I could not get assigned closer. So, after leaving the military I returned to civilian life in the Boston area.

## School of Wicca

Finally, I decided I would show God... and that I would revert to witchcraft and the occult. I was going to the base library and reading books on the occult and the supernatural. There were only a handful of books but they contained a wealth of information. I found an encyclopedia that was a compendium of various religions which included New Age, pagan and occult organizations. It also contained contact information for many of them. I sent out feeler letters, and some got responses with information. After reviewing, I took a correspondence course that offered initiation through the Church and School of Wicca in North Carolina operated by Gavin and Yvonne Frost. The course was twelve lessons, but students wishing to be initiated could complete additional readings, assignments and tasks. I went for initiation and spent the next eighteen months working on this goal. I adopted my "magickal name," Raven. Later, I would attain the elevation of third degree witch and would become known as Lord Raven.

I completed my studies with the Church and School of Wicca in 1991 and was initiated at their Samhain ritual, which we did skyclad (naked) and blindfolded. Standing there in the outer room with my heart beating rapidly... I couldn't believe this night had finally come as I stood there waiting for the ritual to begin. I knew that Yvonne and her husband Gavin were present in the next room and several others who I knew were initiates of the tradition. I waited patiently while they made final preparations for the ceremony. They were casting the circle, invoking the god and goddess and putting everything in place. Finally, one woman led me by the hand into the ritual space. I could smell the rich pungent odor of dragon's blood incense and feel the warmth of candles around me. A soft gentle voice challenged me, "why had I come?" I replied, "To be initiated into the Craft of the wise."

No formal reply was necessary as each person spoke what was in their hearts. They advised me that I could turn back now and all would be well, none would think less of me but if I remained then soon, I would be a witch. "Is that your desire?" I smiled and replied, "With all of my heart." Someone led me forward, and I heard one man performing an incantation as he closed and sealed the circle... an imaginary boundary that surrounded the ritual area. Now we were in a "sacred space"... a world between the worlds. After some instruction they passed me a cup and asked to make a toast. I took the cup of mead in my hands, lifted it high, toasting "to the gods and goddesses and to all the brothers and sisters in the Craft." With a single draught, I swallowed down the entire cup of mead and was told with much amusement that a sip was all that was required and they would have to refill the cup. Apparently it was for everyone to drink from later in the ritual. Gavin laughed, "Well, he has a healthy pagan appetite!" Then the blindfold was removed, and I stood there with the others. Further instruction was given, a time of meditation followed and, much too soon, they concluded the ritual.

For quite a few years I remained part of the organization, and also practiced as a Solitary Witch. At the time, I lived in a tiny attic apartment and could perform rituals freely. I also would make trips up to Salem Massachusetts to celebrate every pagan and Wiccan festival throughout the year.

In 1993 I became involved with the Blue Star tradition of witchcraft and met regularly with a coven in Somerville, Massachusetts. I remained with them for approximately two or three years before returning to solitary practice. As fate happens, I found some other initiates from the Church and School of Wicca were meeting for the eight festivals of the year on Cape Cod. Excited about this news, I joined their group and soon thereafter two more of our group became part of a larger organization... the Black Forest Clan. They were founded by author Silver Ravenwolf, who is known by her many books on witchcraft. Her books raise the eyebrows of many in the Craft because they are "fluffy", but she herself was initiated into British Traditional witchcraft and she could claim a lineage back to Gerald Gardner, the man whose book, "High Magick's Aid," had ignited the whole witchcraft movement in the 20$^{th}$ century.

## The Third Degree

The traditional witchcraft groups, or at least many of them, trace their lineage person by person back to Gerald Gardner, and hence are considered Gardnerian. Silver, who founded the Black Forest Clan, had a direct lineage back to Gardner. I had desired to be a lineage witch, and while at a week long pagan festival in Maryland I met her and once she confirmed that the Church of Wicca had initiated me, she invited me to be part of her group. The jaw-dropping moment for me was when, instead of having to go through the steps of elevations, I could enter as a Third Degree. Weeks later, I traveled to Pennsylvania where the Black Forest Clan conducted their annual gathering; it was there that I was elevated and she passed the power of a third to me in the presence of all the others.

I worked with them for the next several years, and in 1996 I began a Wiccan/pagan study group in my home. We started with a handful of members and after a year we became... The Grotto of the Snow Geese. Some members wanted to follow the path of the Black Forest Clan and to become initiated so we officially affiliated ourselves with Silver's organization.

## The Pinnacle

I was working as a special education teacher at a day program, and one morning before my students arrived I was preparing for the day, and in the lobby I saw a beautiful young woman, looking nervous with a folder full of resumes in her lap. I went over, smiled and introduced myself... and then in the next thirty minutes or so made several other trips to the lobby... anything just to take another look. Eventually we went out together and have been together ever since.

I had several students over the following years, and I was now living with Sharon who was pregnant with my child and studying to become my high priestess in the coven. During my time working with the students I had one attain third degree who ran a coven in Worcester, Massachusetts. There were also several, including Sharon, who attained second degree, qualifying them to serve as high priests or high priestesses. The Grotto of the Snow Geese, and I as their head, became fairly well known and recognized while attending local festivals and throughout Salem.

In the summer of 2009, our coven went to Pennsylvania to attend the annual gathering for the Black Forest Clan. At this gathering, Lady Silver called all third degree witches together for a special meeting. She announced that the Black Forest Clan would become decentralized and instead of her being the head, each third degree running a coven would become a clan head in their own right. It would require us to hold our own annual gathering, known as clan camping's. Spiritually, I felt I had reached the pinnacle of becoming a clan head, responsible for and running two covens in the state.

## Prodigal Programming

But, you know, God has a way of doing things. Even though I had walked away from Him and from the Lord Jesus... He was always there. I'd hear some people mocking Christ which disturbed me and in time I began to think about incorporating Christianity and mixing it with witchcraft. I liked the teachings of Jesus but I was not ready to give up being a witch so, with some apprehension I announced this to my covens. There were people studying Voodoo, Buddhism, New Age and a wide variety of other practices so they just kind of took my announcement with a shrug, with some saying to themselves, "That's just Mike, being Mike!"

I picked up the Bible and reading it from time to time. Being the night owl, I soon gravitated towards watching religious programming on television to the point of even watching the Pope's Christmas Mass! I found myself looking forward to watching the 700 Club or Jimmy Swaggart reruns. To be honest, I often felt the tug in my heart to come back to God but I wasn't ready. I still was carrying a lot of anger and rage, blaming Him for all the things that had gone wrong in my life.

Finally, I found a specific Christian program I couldn't get enough of. The minister was a woman and being a witch I was okay with that. Unlike a lot of the "send me your money" programs that filled the airwaves or programs that were nice but lacked depth, this woman caught my attention. She was teaching the Bible and trained in several languages. She would have a text written out on her whiteboard and then she would write them out in their native language and explain the meanings of the words so that the original intent was clear. She consistently taught that Jesus is God... that He died on the Cross and rose again. It amazed me as each time I watched, it was like the Lord had been fishing, caught me, and was reeling me in on a hook. The show intellectually appealed to me and I tuned in to her program every chance I could.

### Mars Hill

But the Lord wasn't finished with me yet. I had been working at a FedEx call center and there was a co-worker there who was a Christian. We would talk about spiritual things from time to time and thankfully, he wasn't one of those confrontational, "in your face" types. One day they announced that the center was closing and everyone would work from home. Being this was not an option for me, I would have to separate from the company. It was coming up towards Easter in 2009 and he invited me to church with some friends and family. He told me it was at a Calvary Chapel so I asked if it was related to the Calvary Chapel founded by Chuck Smith and he said it was. I went home and told Sharon that I wanted to go to church for Easter so we talked about it and ultimately went.

We went to the service and naturally found it very uncomfortable! We were witches and as far as we were concerned... this was hostile territory. During praise and worship we just kind of stood there listening... not knowing any of the choruses or lyrics. The message was about Jesus rising from the dead and it must have made an impact because on the way home, Sharon and I agreed that we'd go again next week. Little did either of us realize how profoundly we had been affected by our visit as we both felt a tugging at our hearts to return. So strong was this desire, we even considered going down at the next altar call, and over the course of the next several days amazing things were about to happen.

The next Sunday we returned, and the pastor was teaching from the book of Mark (the story of the rich young ruler), when he did something that totally blindsided us. He took us on a rabbit trail and told us to go to the Book of Acts, Chapter 17. We heard about Paul on Mars Hill. To this day I don't remember how he segued from one passage to the other but he did, tying it all together. What was truly mind-blowing was that he had no idea we were there, two pagans who worshiped many gods and goddesses! But there we are, with Paul on Mars Hill... hearing how they had altars to all these different gods and goddesses and then the pastor said, "You are altogether too superstitious!" Whoa... what did he say? Without knowing us or our situation he was quoting this Scripture, and it shocked Sharon and me, knowing God was speaking directly to us. At the end of the message he gave the altar call, and hand in hand, Sharon and I went forward asking him to pray with us so we could receive Christ as our Lord and Savior... to receive forgiveness for our sins, to profess that we believed that He had died for our sins and was raised from the dead. It was utterly amazing.

### The Resignation

The transition out of witchcraft wasn't an especially hard one. I sent Silver a letter of resignation and gave her a report of the condition of the covens. I bestowed to the woman who I had trained to the third degree, my title as clan head and they held a ritual for parting. I think in retrospect that perhaps we should have just broken ties, but that didn't feel right. We explained to all of our contacts in our own covens and Black Forest Clan that we were leaving to follow Christ, and some became nasty in their emails but most were accepting of our decision. Looking back, I am glad I closed that chapter like I did as I have still maintained contact with several Wiccan friends and the door is open for me to share Jesus. Even today on Facebook, there are still Wiccans, and pagans on my personal page which I fill with the gospel message and I know that they see those posts because they often comment on them. The gospel is being preached, and the seed is being planted daily in their hearts of the love and mercy of our great God.

## Full Circle

A year ago, Sharon and I got rid of all our Craft books and paraphernalia. We had bookshelves and file cabinets filled with books, magazines, articles and rituals, so we sat on the living room floor with some trash bags and ripped each book to shreds. I kept a running tally of the cost of the books and it was close to two thousand dollars. Next thing to go was our Craft tools, which included athames (knives), wands, pendants, chalices, and pentacles. Finally, it was time to destroy the statues of gods and goddesses that we had used in worship. Some of them broke easily, while others like our statue of Rhiannon, a Welsh goddess, was very difficult. It was an amazing experience, and it left us feeling like we'd done some serious spiritual housecleaning.

Sharon and I have come full circle. I started out dabbling with witchcraft and got saved before abandoning my faith in a spiritual tantrum that lasted twenty long years till the Lord drew me back and restored me into fellowship with Him. Sharon had joined me on my journey through witchcraft, and though she had not known Christ before, she sure does today. We had once been raising our two young daughters in the Craft, but today they are both saved... and they both love the Lord Jesus.

## In Retrospect

It's important to consider a couple things. First, as a Christian, we are in the Lord's hand and nothing can take us out of His protection... but unfortunately, we can slip out of His hand and when we do that, it is dangerous. If I had died during that time of rebellion I know that I would have gone to hell for eternity and that knowledge was on the horizon of my mind even while I was engaged in witchcraft. We are sinful people... and the only hope we have is that the Lord is more faithful than we are! It was HIS faithfulness and not mine that brings me here today. Also, it is vital to understand the role that prayer played in our coming out of witchcraft.

## The Greatest Thing

Today we serve at the same Calvary Chapel where we got saved and we are growing in the Lord's Word there. When people hear my testimony they do one of two things: they become distant as though I am carrying leprosy, or they are enthralled by the Lord's amazing grace.

The greatest thing ever in my life was not being a third degree witch, being able to perform rituals and spells that worked... being talented as a tarot reader or running two covens. The greatest thing in my life is that the Lord God of the universe saw me in my rebellion and sin and yet loved me still. He came and became a baby, born of a virgin and lived a pure and sinless life. He died on the Cross to pay for my sins and then He rose again. As a witch I worshiped and followed many gods and goddesses. I got involved in witchcraft because it promised freedom, power, and pleasure. It promised sexual liberty, and it promised happiness. Initially, it brought these things into my life, but they soon became empty. The gods and goddesses proved to be untrustworthy, and all the benefits witchcraft promised had vanished. They were like a mist, here for a moment then faded away. But the Lord God who created the universe is alive in me... and I am alive in Him. My name is Michael. I used to be a witch but now I serve Him alone.

# CHAPTER NINE

―⁂―

# Lupe King

*Lupe was born with a gift that neither her family nor church understood, but years later this ability would label her as a natural-born witch who would quickly elevate from initiate to a third degree high priestess in the heart of Salem, Massachusetts. Then one night she had a dream that would reveal the battle over her soul.*

My name is Lupe King, and I was born in a small town in rural West Texas. My parents had seven children... I was the fifth of three girls and four boys.

As a young child of four or five, I was incredibly precocious. I loved the wind, sun, tree, flowers, moon, and all the creatures; winged, furry, four footed, two footed, and everything else that existed that spoke "Life." Rain, rainbows, lightning and thunder were big on my radar. Being from the southwest, I particularly loved the whistling sound of sand storms!

My spirit was thrilled at all these things. I'd spend hours conversing with creation and felt creation was alive, both animate and inanimate, as it responded to my expressions of love and desire for oneness with it.

### The Scapegoat

As I grew older, I started to recognize problems at home and in retrospect I now see it had been something that had always been there but because of my innocence I did not acknowledge it. My father drank heavily and my mother was always the object of his wrath in one way or another. This affected us as children and alcoholism ran rampant in most of us later on as adults.

I remember bringing home test papers and art projects from school and Mom giving me props and then putting them up on the refrigerator. By the time I was in the third grade my mother's attitudes and behaviors began to turn. She became angry, mean, and unlovable. The issues of abandonment and rejection came in like a flood.

Racism was prominent in the school systems then, permeated by daily emotional cruelty with anyone not of the white culture or the same social status. Battles at home with verbal and physical abuse, battles at school via verbal taunting and being the butt of cruel jokes was no way for any child to grow-up, but it happened.

At the young ages of six and up, we (myself and siblings) were forced to work at 5:00 a.m. before school and after school from 4 p.m. to sundown and even sometimes on Saturday till noon. We hoed, picked cotton, and moved irrigation pipes. Back then, ranchers needed to be in the big bucks in order to afford such equipment as the Electronic Rolling Wheel irrigation systems; so we supplied almost everything the job required in human strength, agility, and stamina. Being children of Hispanic farmers in rural, racist Texas is not something many people have survived and still maintained a healthy mindset.

By the age of nine, abuse had been in my life for at least three years. My mom, being unable to express or vent her anger towards my father, lashed out at me instead as I became the "chosen one" for her displaced anger. Shame and low self-esteem flooded my life, and thus the scapegoat was birthed.

Some things were good in my life; I met my best friend, Luz, in first grade. Luz's mother visited us on and off for about three years and I had no clue she was Christian. My father, when not in a drunken stupor, was actually a good man, which puzzled me as it was like living with Dr. Jekyll and Mr. Hyde.

At ten I was sexually abused, and self-hatred entered into my heart because of it. As these horrendous things were happening to me, I lost trust in humanity and I started to lean more on creation as its creatures became my best friends and family.

## The Bruja

I started to grow in sensitivity of the unseen realm as I would weep over the unspoken pain of those that were ill and in the physical realm, my heart would break over puppies that died. My mother who never understood my spiritual gifts started to call me "weird, a bad omen, and bruja" (witch).

Sometimes I would just know things, almost like a second sense and I would share them with Mom. I guess I just wanted her to love me and thought she might appreciate my gift of knowledge because at this point the beatings became really, really, bad. I'd show up at school with cuts and bruises and nobody even questioned it because there was no Social Services and it didn't help that my brothers and father had gained a reputation of being regional terrors. I believe people just looked the other way.

## The Shunning

My friend Luz's mother was still visiting on and off and one day she invited our family to visit her church, my parents agreed and thus, "church going" started to become a way of life. Shortly after, my father accepted Christ and amazingly stopped drinking and smoking overnight! He never drank or smoked again and I have always seen this as a miracle. Before long, with both promptings from The Holy Spirit and my father, we all accepted Christ and were baptized.

You would think that by getting to this point, everything was roses for the rest of my life and that would have been nice, but not so!

Ironically, the beatings continued and sexual abuse still threatened me. I relentlessly battled to defend my honor and life. My parents were oblivious to what was going on and I already felt unloved, beaten, and blamed for everything, so if anyone found out about the sexual abuse, I definitely felt I would meet my demise.

As we continued to be "Sunday Christians," my father became deacon of the church. It wasn't long before I started to let my gifts shine but sadly, soon after, I was called into an elder's meeting and was told I needed to stop telling people about themselves and their issues because I was frightening them as they believed it was ungodly. I stopped for a season but I could not contain the incredible gifting within me and started to do as my nature dictated; share.

Once again I was called in as my father sat in as deacon; he never once stood up and defended me just as he never once defended me from my mother. He was silent as the accusations of witchcraft and divination came forth... I was cast out from the church and shunned by all.

## The New, Calloused Me

By this time I'm fifteen and have been experiencing guardians that were showing up from the unseen realm. I never really felt lonely as I gave myself in friendship to them and they responded.

By the time I turned seventeen I had long since been engaging in witchcraft arts and occultism, via books and magazines.

I remember reaching out to my mother one day and she pushed me away so hard that I almost fell over. I remember giving her one hard look and said to myself, "You don't love me, and so I don't love you either!" Something really seemed to have entered my soul as I felt my heart harden, literally as a new, calloused personality took over.

By now they have cast me out of the church for about two years, beatings are still happening and had gotten worse because I now defended myself. The last time it happened, I almost died yet no one took me to a hospital for treatment but I was nurtured back to health by my own abusers...WHY??? I honestly don't know! I only know I decided to leave home as I figured it would be better if I was to die at the hands of a stranger than by the hands of those that were supposed to love me. "The world may be kinder," I thought. After leaving, I was homeless for a while. Any place where I could lay my head at night was home until morning and I learned most people were kind, some gave me food and sometimes money.

It was rough going as I was never sure where I would end up next. Soon I wound up in New York City and worked as a nanny for about a year.

Finally, I met my first husband and fell into young love. After a while I felt the need to reconnect with people back home and let them know where I was, since no one heard from me for about a year. I wrote a letter, and it was well received; I made my journey back with future husband intact.

I was no longer the naïve, sweet, loving kid I used to be. I resolved not to take any crap from anyone. I had continued my journey with the occult and had learned how to use the supernatural to my advantage.

I vowed never to allow myself to be hurt again and certainly not to be used sexually by some demented mind. I would warn people, "I have a Craft and I know how to use it!"

Anger was the shield of protection I returned with and there must have been something my mother and others saw in me, because I was never messed with again.

I was angry with God. I blamed Him for everything that had ever happened to me and I especially blamed Him for having horrible and evil children with my rationale being, "You have horrible and evil children... You must be a horrible and evil Father."

After that it seemed I just kept going deeper and deeper into the occult and witchcraft. I had some terrible experiences while in Texas, one of which I was attacked by some terrible people and was hospitalized and almost died. I was laid up for about six months as my body healed quickly but the incident traumatized my mind and I nearly gave up hope. After much time in therapies of all kinds, I could go home and shortly after that we left Texas for the last time.

## The Mentor

Hubby and I landed in Massachusetts and of all places... Salem, otherwise known as "The Witchcraft Capital of the World." After fifteen years of marriage and three children, our marriage soured because of my ex-husband's infidelity and, unbeknownst to me, my negligence and inability to forgive. Feeling isolated, vulnerable and seeking a meaning for my life, I believed it was finally time for me to seek out my destiny.

It was at this precise moment I submerged myself fully into the Craft. Salem is where I met my mentor and high priest, a well-known name in witchcraft. He was also a "Once upon a time, Christian." We shared stories about how we had been mistreated and not understood by God or His family. We shared our pains, sorrows and seemed of one mind about life. He witnessed many times when I knew beforehand what he was going to say, or I would answer questions without first reading the occult books or study materials. He told me I was a natural-born witch and said, "It's inside you! It's in your blood, it's in your soul... and because of this you would be great in Wicca." Witchcraft gave me an identity, self-worth and a sense of family I never had. They accepted me and we became close.

I was in a fast moving spiral into the Craft and started to ascend in Wiccan levels from initiation to initiation, from apprentice to high priestess, eventually creating my own coven. We were meeting on full moons, new moons, and all Sabbats for teaching, receiving wisdom from the "Old Ones," and for hands' on magickal works and spell castings.

I lived at a neighborhood called "The Point" in Salem, away from Wiccan friends and my mentor. I was watching my personal story unfolding as the Hispanic population gravitated towards the spiritual aspects of witchcraft and came regularly for tarot readings and spell workings in their lives. It was not uncommon for me to come home to find surprise "gifts" left at my doorstep by thankful patrons.

## Enter Peter

Eventually, the marriage would end in divorce. I had a mile-long trail of unforgiveness and an even longer trail of desire for retribution with me being both judge and jury.

A year passed, and I was able to close the door to my fifteen-year-old marriage. Ten years of the relationship were good, but the last five were painful, disastrous, and destructive. I met my current husband Peter as we worked at the same plant that made, of all things, Ouija Boards. I dressed in the "Starched Blacks" that Salem witches are known for, with a pentacle (the occult symbol for protection amidst other things), with a garnet at its center.

Peter, who was my boss at a particular job at the plant shared knowledge about stones and their properties which every New Age Practitioner is into and soon became a friend. He was in the throes of his own marriage gone bad and divorce was in the makings.

## Brought Before The Council

In the meantime, jealousy raised its ugly head amidst other leaders in the Craft over my quick ascension into levels of witchcraft. Complaints about Wiccan laws arose, and they brought me before The Council along with my mentor, who found loopholes in the laws so I would not be disciplined.

Laws regarding the Christian God were discussed as I had incorporated Jesus and His angels into my circle castings because of "my" friend who had been spoon-feeding me Jesus for almost a year and unbeknownst to me had two churches praying for my salvation... Jesus was quickly recovering ground.

My mentor and I escaped The Council's wrath by the skin of our teeth, however, other incidents quickly followed as my confusion with The Christian God and the many gods of Wicca grew like a fungus.

I started to doubt many things and was challenging my mentor continually. I couldn't understand why Wicca allowed us as many gods as we wanted, yet there seemed to be a problem with

The One Christian God. It seemed no answer was good enough, and they told me that as long as I used Jesus like all the other gods it would be okay. I was however, warned to tread lightly because the spiritual forces were not content with sharing their ground with The Christian God.

Things got more complicated as more was being asked of me as I continued to ascend levels and was told, "You have learned the good, now you must also learn the bad!"

Necromancy was no big deal for me! I was always conversing with disembodied souls but was told that in order to continue ascending in the Craft I must raise a dead body, which was way out of my league. It was not why I had gone into witchcraft and felt I was being setup by the Council. My only thought was, "Raise a dead body, only God can do that!" I was not about to give the Council and its allies what they wanted since they were only waiting for me to slip.

Things quickly got darker and darker as I soon realized that the levels in witchcraft hierarchy had slowly, yet progressively, reached a point of no return. If I had engaged in raising a dead body, I would have crossed a line from witchcraft to sorcery, from white magick to black magick, and from Wicca to Satanism.

I reminded myself that this was not my goal or desire. All I ever wanted was to be loved, happy, accepted, and to have the ability to defend myself while helping others.

## Battle Over My Soul

Rituals started to go bad as spirit guides wanted to do their own thing. I saw their true manifestations, which were not angels of light or beautiful winged fairy creatures. There was not enough fairy dust in the seen or unseen realm to mask what they really looked like.

My coven had become fearful with stepping into portals of different dimensions, and astral projection had become more dangerous than we bargained for. Reality for me had become an issue as I could not tell the difference with what was real and what was surreal. One night I had the most vivid dream... I stood between my mentor and Peter, my then close friend from work. They were both pulling me in opposite directions, one on each arm. I thought they would tear me in two. Darkness surrounded me except for a light from above. I saw my high priest's angry face while Peter remained calm. When I shared my dream with Peter, he advised me not to go with either him or my mentor, but go to the light. His eyes filled with tears as he spoke, knowing they were not his words but the Holy Spirit's. My times with Jesus were quickly becoming a healing balm as I started to gravitate more and more to the safety and peace of His presence.

Months later I was still in the Craft but had isolated myself into practicing solitary. I worked alone, while checking in from time to time with my mentor. Months later through an incredible encounter Jesus came to me. It was during a ritual at midnight, on a lighthouse pier surrounded by the ocean, He came unexpectedly and I battled Him, yet He would not give way. He was persistent... all the anger and rage bottled up inside of me exploded against Him as my heart broke when I tangibly felt His strong and loving arms around me and He spoke nothing else except, "I love you!" His presence was great and I could not deny it. After hours of crying and letting all the years of my pain out, I concluded that it was time for me to leave the Craft.

### The Sabbatical

Leaving was difficult. When I presented myself to Council, I informed them I needed time away and was considering leaving Wicca. They tried to reassure me by saying I was just tired and needed time to think, so they granted me a sabbatical of a year and a day and they expected me to come back. I left knowing I would never return.

For a year my now husband Peter and I searched for a church along the North Shore that was gifted in spiritual warfare but found none that were appropriately equipped to take on the battles that would come knocking on their doors once I became a member. It was only God that took up the slack and filled in the voids where these churches failed and as I read His Word, His Spirit taught me. My lack of trust of Christians was one of the hardest things I had to deal with and it didn't help with our search. I knew in my heart this anger towards God's children needed to end and I needed to forgive them as He had forgiven me. It took years to get to this place, but I finally did! It is important to know that when one has been wounded by one church family; it is only God's love through another church family that will bring healing.

We found a small, simple, and humble church in Beverly whose people were loving, kind and willing to help in any way they could. Most important of all, I felt safe and accepted. Love was great in this little church and although they were not knowledgeable in spiritual warfare as many aren't, His love releases healing in all the right places of our spirit, mind, and body thus we remained there for many years.

### The Battle Rages On

The two years that followed leaving the Craft, was a time of great spiritual battles; phone calls in the middle of the night were relentless, occult gifts left at my door or mailbox, threats to my children's lives and endless nightmares... all initiated from my past occult world. In my personal walk I battled daily with old mindsets and behaviors and the pull to return to former ways, wavering between Christianity and the Occult. Physically, both my husband and I acquired ailments that were medically unaccounted for but vanished once we were prayed over. Moments of physical stagnation; I went through periods where I physically could not move or lost my breath. In the battle's heat, God taught me that most of what I encountered was physical manifestations of a demonic presence. As revelation through His Word came, I was freed from all torment and oppression.

### New Life in Him

It has now been twenty-two years since leaving the Craft and, in time, God has restored all that was lost or stolen. I remarried Christian and we've been married almost seventeen years. We own our home, and my children, which were temporarily taken from me via the system, were returned shortly afterwards. So, with my husband's three children from his previous marriage, we have raised a total of six and they are all grown up, some are married with their own families and some are single and living on their own. We have a myriad of grandchildren, both biological and spiritual, of all diverse ages.

We were at that tiny, loving church for years and still visit and maintain our relationships with them. They are still champions in love and compassion who minister to the broken areas of all that come.

The time came when growth and maturity reached its fullness for us there and we lovingly said goodbye and moved on.

We now attend an incredible Apostolic Church and although our numbers are small, our faith and love for God is great. We move in the area of the supernatural realms of God as my gifts continue to grow and multiply as I use them for His kingdom alone.

## My Forever Prayer

Now all has been laid out bare before God and men concerning my testimony. Had my upbringing by my family and society not been so harsh or had the church not been so blinded and deceived by legalism, religion or witchcraft, the enemy would not have had such a field day with my life.

Ultimately, witchcraft was in my life because I made the choice to walk in it, either by ignorance and deception, but the church failed to do its part, by not walking in the righteousness of Christ, by not entertaining the many gifts of the Spirit, both practical and supernatural, by leaving out God's Spoken (prophetic) Word, and by expounding upon The Law without balancing it out with the love that "holds no account of wrongs" (1 Corinthians 13).

May we as a Church... love, do not criticize, judge or condemn. Do not be afraid or pull away from witches, they are part of God's creation and they have hearts and souls like yours.

It is my "forever" prayer that the Church would arise by the blood of Christ and take back the ground lost through ignorance, arrogance, and the mixing of the Holy with the profane. That it would meet the spiritual guidelines of the resplendent Bride. Be blessed!

# CHAPTER TEN

## Selah Ally Tower

I *(Selah Ally) embarked on a spellbinding journey into the ways of magick and witchcraft for over a decade. An initiated Witch, I had just completed my training to become high priestess when, just short of my elevation ritual, I had an encounter that would change my perception of God forever.*

To me, God was way up in the clouds and it would take death to meet Him, or so my young mind thought. I grew up hearing my first Bible stories in Sunday school at the Episcopal church my family attended. As a young child, God had given me sensitivity in the spirit, and I soon learned that He was within hearing distance when my sister and I prayed for our ailing grandfather on his deathbed and he continued to live throughout the length of our prayers. Then as children often do, we became preoccupied with other things and stopped praying. Grandpa slipped peacefully to his heavenly home, and as solemn and confusing as that was for me, I had this strange excitement that brought God closer to my world; however, neither my sister nor my family shared this concept.

While my parents were raising me in the Anglican Christian faith, I also heard stories of another spiritual dimension retold by my grandmother. My mother's mother often spoke of my great-aunt, Gracie, who at the time was a reverend of a nearby Spiritualist church.

One account she often shared was of Gracie's early years

reading the tarot and a man who refused to heed the advice she had given him. Grandmom conveyed how the innocent victim had been found hanging from an old iron fence, dead, in what they determined a freak accident. This instilled both fear and a morbid curiosity in me at the same time. Many times, my grandmother would tell stories only to stop short of the climactic ending, saying it was not something for my young ears to hear, but I wanted to know more.

### The Other Side of the Mirror

At a young age, I had what my parents called an imaginary friend that appeared in the mirror of my mother's bedroom. She had a dark countenance and darker hair than mine. I would spend hours hidden away with my friend on the other side of the mirror, and her daunting presence and self-assured composure intrigued me. At the time I did not know that neither she nor the other strangers who would visit me in my growing-up years were actually from the spirit world, and that my imaginary friend was in fact a spirit guide. I first discovered their origin years later when I learned meditation in my witchcraft studies.

### Poppet Magick

When I was around twelve, I got in a cat fight with my best friend, which sent her college-aged sister banging on my door. I sought revenge in the back of my long, narrow closet with a small dark-haired doll as my poppet (a doll created to represent a person for the purpose of sympathetic magick). I was clueless as I positioned pins and wrapped the doll with a string from waist to thigh to close her womb. The words that came from my lips were unknown to me and not something I had picked up on television or read in a book.

I soon forgot about the bound doll in the back of my closet, but my friend and I resumed our friendship. At the time, I did not fully understand that I had just engaged in the practice of the dark arts, nor did I have knowledge of Scripture that would have warned of its practice, but that did not prevent the spell from going forth. (Ezekiel 13:17–23 warns against sewing charms used in connection with magickal practices.) The charm bound around the doll had an evil intent of harm attached to it, but I had not realized its repercussions until many years later when my friend suffered from infertility. Thank God, she received prayer to break the spell and soon after gave birth of a healthy baby boy.

## Tract of Salvation

I entered my teen years in the generation of peace, love, and flower power. That flew the coop where parents and authority figures were concerned, as I became the militant rebel. My eighth grade teacher had a major impact on my spiritual life when, after I was outed by a friend for passing notes, she read my mind-altering poetry in front of the entire class. Soon afterward, and out of what I believe was concern for me, she shared the truth of the living Christ with me after class. That night I went home and said the sinner's prayer off the back page of the evangelistic tract she had given to me. The school year ended and that summer I received a surprise package in the mail. It was a Good News Bible from my teacher, Miss Jackson, but try as I might to read it, I did not spiritually grasp it and the Bible took up residence in a box in my closet.

## Jesus at Giants Stadium

At twenty, I finally caved and went with my best friend's sister, now a crazed Jesus freak, to Giants Stadium for a Jesus crusade. It was my first experience with contemporary worship and this new prayer language being spoken by thousands beneath the open sky. After returning home, I recommitted my life to Jesus and returned to the Episcopal church with a desire to share my newfound spiritual enthusiasm. I taught Sunday school and became a youth group advisor. To satisfy my spiritual thirst, I went to the Assemblies of God Church on Sunday and Wednesday evenings.

## Match Made in Heaven

After a few years, a friend invited me to a nondenominational church, New Zion Christian Fellowship, that had a ministry in healing and deliverance. It was at the pastor and his wife's dining room table that I first met my future husband, Michael. We dated for a year before we planned our wedding day. It seemed this indeed was a match made in heaven. Our first year of marriage seemed perfect in every way; Michael was a sensitive and caring husband who put most men to shame. But soon after we started a family, my ideal husband withdrew and over the next several years our marriage plunged into a downward spiral that no amount of counseling, prayer, or fasting could stop.

## The Strange Debate

I was eight months pregnant when I ended up at the bottom of my staircase with my head in a pool of blood. I have no recollection of how I got there and can only describe the supernatural experience of looking down at my motionless body. At first, I was a spectator to a strange conversation until someone directed a question at me. I scarcely remember what they asked, but my answer was clear: "No, I don't want to leave my children."

It seemed I was in the middle of a supernatural debate, but after receiving an inner sense of security for my children and being warned I would endure suffering, pain, and even venture into the Opponent's camp, my answer remained the same. Only God knows what happened and from where this mysterious conversation and forewarning had originated. At the time, it was unimaginable for me to think I would ever walk away from Jesus!

My pastor brushed the entire event off as an attack from the Enemy and advised me to ignore the spiritual implications that had occurred because it could not possibly have been from God. For the next six years I repressed this harrowing episode in the back of my mind; after all, I was devoted to Jesus and my Christian faith.

My marriage continued to deteriorate, and we walked around the house on eggshells in fear of my husband's emotional episodes. At times he was silent and withdrawn, but in an instant he would become irritated, angry, and occasionally even violent. Years would go by before they diagnosed him as bipolar, giving at least an explanation for his erratic behavior.

## Forbidden Fruit

It appeared God had turned a deaf ear to my pleas for my marriage, financial security, and even basic needs, as my husband quit work, attempting to raise our family on a disability check. To make matters worse, I felt abandoned by God since I no longer heard His voice. Just as Eve did in the garden of Eden, I had begun to doubt God's Word as true and relevant in my life.

But it did not stop there. Doubt quickly led to unbelief, and it was not long before I questioned the Bible altogether. Unknowingly, I was now in a vulnerable position, as the Enemy had me exactly where he wanted me—paralyzed in unbelief—and my faltering faith had become fertile soil for compromise.

Ironically, a book that was supposed to be a warning about the dangers of the occult was the source that sparked my curiosity and led to my library search to research the subject. The fall of mankind was being replayed in the garden of my own backyard, and I, as Eve, had bitten into its forbidden fruit of knowledge, believing that God had kept me from receiving power and blessings. My great sin was neither eating the apple nor the knowledge it provided, but rather disobeying God.

Then one night my research progressed into action as I beheld the enchantment of the full moon that beckoned me outside my window. I stood beneath its glow and called upon the goddess. Energy flowed through me, and when I went back inside, my children questioned why my face seemed to be illuminated. I knew at that point that it had opened a passage to an ancient way of life.

## Ancient Ways

The next day I came across a magazine and could not believe my eyes when I found an ad for those seeking the ancient path of witchcraft. I immediately sent my request, and within the next month had begun my studies with The Church and School of Wicca, the first Wiccan organization to have obtained the status as an officially recognized religion. Flamen (High Priest) Gavin was my instructor, and I chose the initiatory part of the course.

A year and a day later, I went from studying about the Craft to becoming a practitioner.

I desired more, but to pick up and move to the school in North Carolina was out of the question, so I focused my magick on finding a coven closer to home. Cerridwen's Cauldron appeared in a newspaper article, and I made my way to check out this local witch shop. I became a regular and before long was invited to my first ritual with the coven.

By then, New Zion Christian Fellowship had applied Matthew 18, or shunning, which they used as discipline. This was meant to bring me back into the fold, but it had a reverse effect and gave me more time to focus my energy on occult practices and pagan friendships. It may seem hypocritical, but I was deeply hurt that people who were once as close as a family now avoided me.

### Reincarnation of a Salem Execution

Next on my agenda was Salem, Massachusetts, known for the witch trials of 1692, where I took a fall excursion with a few Wiccan friends. I had a rather unusual experience when we visited the Old Burying Point Cemetery. A woman appeared out of nowhere, looked me straight in the eyes, and addressed me by the name of a woman who had been executed during the Salem witch trials. Ironically, I believed I was her reincarnation and had returned to live out the fate of what they had accused me of. As quickly as the woman appeared, she vanished.

### Wicca: A Way of Life

I would spend the next decade working with the coven, and at times when the coven was on hiatus, I would practice solitary. We met at new and full moons, furthering our growth in magickal abilities, and celebrated the eight Sabbats. To me, Wicca was more than just a religion; it was a way of life. Treading its path began at sunrise and continued through my dreams at night.

Every year my coven held an annual Witch's Ball, which was an event open to both pagans and the public. During the year we held drum circles, went to pagan gatherings, and attended exclusive coven rituals in the mountains. Notable authors and Craft elders taught at the shop my high priestess ran and occasionally gathered around our campfire at pagan festivals. They initiated me into the Craft, and I continued my studies through my progression of elevations, which is advancement to higher degrees. Becoming a high priestess of my own coven was my ultimate destiny.

## "Who Do You Say That I Am?"

I was totally enchanted by the ways of magick when I was rocked to my core by being awakened one night to the face of Jesus. His eyes pierced right through me as He asked a simple question: "Who do you say that I am?"

I jumped up from this seemingly tangible nightmare, but I couldn't shake that face—those eyes that lay my soul bare. Three times I tried to go back to sleep only to hear His vivid voice asking the same gripping question until I finally shouted, "I don't know, but I'll find out!"

The eerie silence lingered in my bedroom and the back of my mind as I tried to repress it from my memory, but there was no doing that. Months would go by before I finally contacted my now ex-pastor, wanting to hear a confirmation that it could not have possibly come from God. My hope was soon dashed and my fears substantiated, as I had to settle for the harsh realization that God would still talk to me.

What really troubled my soul the most was the question He directed at me. Christians consider Jesus the Savior, and witches consider Him a teacher or a prophet, but the question He asked was not for Christians or witches. It was for me, and with that, I was invited back to church to search for the answer I had promised I would seek.

## Egyptian Vagabond

For the next year I straddled the fence between church and coven. I can only describe the struggle within as my soul as being torn in two. God continued to speak through prophetic dreams and Scripture as I searched for my answer. One morning while I was still in a semiconscious, surreal state, I saw a newsletter before me with some kind of cartoon-like drawing of an Egyptian vagabond on it. On the top was the heading "The Last Days Newsletter." It seemed familiar, but I could not quite place it until I remembered the name Keith Green. He had once been my favorite Christian music artist, and his ministry had put out the newsletter.

As strange as it may seem, I could not recall even one of his songs, not a line or melody. How could I remember "Puff the Magic Dragon" from my childhood, but be unable to come up with music that had such an impact on my life? It was as though someone had erased it from my memory. Determined, I drove to the nearest Christian bookstore, bought a Keith Green CD, put it in the car stereo, and hit play.

All the words I once knew by heart came back to me as I drove home in tears. Something inside was stirring, and I realized the dream had led me right to the songs that would be instrumental in my pursuit.

### Eternity without God

With my interest in re-exploring God piquing, I faced my next excommunication from the church, but this time it was not only for my pagan ways but also because of what they saw as an inappropriate relationship with a Christian friend, Bo, before a divorce. I concluded that Jesus was the Son of God, but it did not change the fact I was a witch, and after facing what I considered their unwarranted rejection, I became enraged and even more determined to turn away from God and delve deeper into magick.

Over the next several years I became intolerant of Christians and anything to do with Christianity. I even accepted the concept of spending eternity without God, as I believed the day was coming when I would fulfill my mission in helping others who had survived an apocalypse in what I can only describe as a parallel last-days scenario. It seemed biblical end-times teachings were matching up with some noted pagan prophesy in planning for survival during an upcoming worldwide catastrophe, and I was content choosing the latter. While I thought I had spiritually progressed, I had reached an all-time spiritual low.

## Banished

The one thing that still irked me was the spiritual ties with my ex-pastor. I often contemplated what he had taught, and it angered me because it hindered my progression in the Craft. I decided this parental spiritual bond had to be broken, so I brought my relationship with my spiritual father before the coven in a banishing ritual to break any ties. The next moon cycle, I contacted him to check on the result of the spell, and reality hit hard when I learned that he was retiring from the ministry and moving out of state. I was plagued with extreme sorrow and guilt, questioning what I had done.

One of the hardest things I have ever had to do was to pick up the phone and tell him what I had done. Even more heartbreaking was hearing his hurtful response. I realized that, in my blind-sightedness, I had gotten what I asked for and he would soon be out of my life. But God had another plan.

A few weeks later I got a call. My spiritual father was inviting me to church to meet an ex-occultist. I really had no desire to meet her, but after what I had done, I felt obligated to go. In what should have been the last place in the world I would want to be at the night after our Samhain ritual, there I was in church.

## You Can't Run from God

The first thing I remember is a woman of African descent giving me a big hug, but her words seemed surreal to me. "God loves you," she said as I silently decided she was just responding with the hospitality protocols and really had no clue she was saying this to a witch.

Worship became my tear-fest, baffled as I was; after all, life was good. The pastor announced his sermon title, and of course it had to be on Halloween. I was just about to get up and leave when the woman who had hugged me came back and said, "You're going to think this crazy, but God told me to come hold your hand," and that is exactly what she did!

Not wanting to be rude, I sunk into my seat, infuriated by the sermon being preached. At last, the pastor was finished bashing my belief, and with that, my newfound friend retreated to her original seat. I thought I could bear this to the end of the service, until the pastor engaged the church in spiritual warfare, which was my cue to get out. I was not quick enough, and the ex-occultist intercepted my exit. We talked, and the next thing I knew, not only had the warfare ended, but the entire church had cleared out and I found myself barricaded between a bookcase enclosure and a wall of spiritual warriors.

When their praying turned into what I considered attack mode, I'd had enough and attempted to leave, but they only prayed harder, so I literally ditched underneath the arms of the man blocking my exit and escaped out the door. That would have been the end of the story except that in my hurry I forgot my purse and car keys. I re-entered with caution, carefully scoping out an opening to exit, but Pastor Lyndon in his soft-spoken voice said, "You can't run from God," and I stopped dead in my tracks. The warfare ceased, at least the outward expression of it, and I sat down with the pastor and had a long discussion that ended with my giving my life back to Jesus.

That was the beginning of the long and winding road back. Wicca was far more than a religious belief; I had lived, breathed, and trod upon a magickal path that did not dissipate because of my decision. Magick was everywhere—in every sunrise, every moon phase, and throughout the natural world. What was even more difficult was that nothing had sent me running in the opposite direction; I simply had encountered the greater love of God and could not say no to Him. My walk out would teach me what grace was really all about.

## Even in the Darkest Places

Sometimes temptation got the best of me and I would go to ritual. On one such occasion, I stood in circle when an enormous tongue of fire pierced the middle of our sacred space and it seemed no one else saw it but me. Ritual that night could not have ended quickly enough, but what happened next would completely throw me off guard: one covenor approached and shared how I had been a source of hope during a difficult time in her life. She explained how she saw strength, fire, wisdom, and compassion in my eyes, and I quickly realized the eyes she described were not mine, but the eyes of Jesus.

It was then that Psalm 139:7 came to life: "Where can I go from Your Spirit? Or where can I flee from Your presence? If I ascend into heaven, You are there; If I make my bed in hell, behold, You are there. If I take the wings of the morning, and dwell in the uttermost parts of the sea, even there Your hand shall lead me, and Your right hand shall hold me."

I finally got it! So many years before, I had believed the lie that God had abandoned me, and now I realized that He had never left me; in fact, He was with me even in the depths of darkness.

I filled a box with my books, robes, magickal tools, and paraphernalia, and drove to my pastor's house. He met me by the fire pit and added another log to the glowing flames. We emptied the box, and its contents became the fuel to the flames that consumed them. When the fire had died down, I took my Book of Shadows and tossed it into the hot embers, which burst into an orange-red glow. I watched all of my magickal workings, spells, and rituals go up in smoke and prayed for a godly semblance of order in my life.

## Full Circle

I knew I had come full circle after my daughter's friend showed up at our door with Children's Services, in need of a place to stay. Without a second thought I welcomed this victimized teenage girl into my heart and home. But it was not long before I realized there was much more to her innocent destruction than met the eye; she was an extremely troubled soul.

Shortly after her overenthusiastic entrance into our home, I realized her turmoil went beyond the emotional level, as she was dabbling with dark magick. At first I refused to even consider having her removed from our home, knowing all too well the result of my subjection to the church's rebuke, but this was not entirely a spiritual decision. After I learned that my family was actually in physical danger and discovered what I believed to be a potential murderous plot, I made another difficult decision and had Children's Services find her a new home.

## Breaking Idols

After a sermon on 1 Samuel—about the Israelites disobeying the voice of God and, rather than destroying everything, sparing the king and the best possessions—I was moved to go home and make sure my house was spiritually swept. I went into the basement and gathered all of my foster daughter's remaining magickal possessions, along with a few of my own that I had missed burning in my pastor's fire pit, and called Bo. We drove to the river's edge and conveniently found a concrete slab, possibly the remains of a boat ramp.

Bo, by no means a small man, was the first to take the sledgehammer to the metal, but the goddess-sculpted dagger did not break. Yet when I slammed the hammer down, it shattered into pieces. Once all were broken, we threw them into their riverbed grave. Deuteronomy 12:3-4 describes how God instructed the Israelites to destroy all their idols, and in essence symbolically reject pagan deities. We too show our rejection of pagan idolatry by discarding these images and, in essence, proclaiming our devotion in following God.

As I gazed across the river, Exodus 13:17-18 came to mind. God had taken the Israelites the roundabout way to avoid the confrontation He knew they were not able to handle. It seemed my life had taken a similar road and God had brought me in a roundabout way to where I stood that day. The way had been made clear for me to cross to the other side, and, like the Red Sea, the river waters consumed any remaining elements of my pagan past.

As I turned to walk away, I held onto the assurance of Romans 8:38–39: "For I am persuaded that neither death nor life, nor angels nor principalities nor powers, nor things present nor things to come, nor height nor depth, nor any other created thing, shall be able to separate us from the love of God which is in Christ Jesus our Lord."

## Relentless Love

In hindsight, I now see the subtle deception that lured me off God's chosen path. It took years for me to discover what I share with you now, which is that we are never beyond hope with God. It does not matter where we are in our life or how far we have strayed; He is right there waiting for us with open arms. There is nothing and no one that can separate us from His love, not even ourselves. His heart longs for us, and He desires for all to be restored to fellowship with Him. Why wander in the desert when He will part the waters leading to the Promised Land?

*Read the full-length testimony of Selah Ally Tower (S. A. Tower) in her debut book, Taken from the Night—A Witch's Encounter with God, available at most major retail bookstores. To learn more, go to www.takenfromthenight.com.*

# FROM THE CRAFT TO CHRIST

# CHAPTER ELEVEN

## Victoria Shephard

Victoria had a God-shaped hole she attempted to fill through New Age spirituality and ultimately Wicca. Over the next five years she became part of a coven, was initiated into the Craft and wrote articles for several pagan publications. What started out as a simple trip to purchase a tape at a concert would turn into an unanticipated, life-changing event.

My first contact with the gospel occurred at Reno Christian Academy when I was about four years old. I was there for less than a year as my parents pulled me out because I was asking uncomfortable questions such as, "Why we didn't go around ringing doorbells to tell people about Jesus just like my teacher did?"

When I was about ten years old, my mom and I occasionally attended the Seventh-day Adventist Church in a nearby town. The Adventist Church was very legalistic back then, though at the time I had no concept of what that meant. I thought of myself as a Christian though I had never had a conversion experience or asked Jesus into my heart. I'm not even sure I ever heard the gospel explained to me. I gave intellectual assent to the truth that Jesus was the Son of God who came to die for my sins, but I didn't have a personal relationship with Him. This was not a saving faith, for the Bible says that "even the demons believe... and tremble," (James 2:19).

### Why I Left the Church

The turning point toward disaster came when I borrowed a

sermon tape from the church library. The tape basically said that Christians never sin. They probably used Scripture references such as I John 5:18 - "We know that no one born of God sins," but this is a poor translation. What it actually means in the Greek is that no one born of God continues in sin, that is, a truly saved person cannot live in continuing sin.

It does not mean that a saved person never sins, for 1 John 1:8 says, "If we say that we have no sin, we are deceiving ourselves and the truth is not in us." First John 1:9 starts off, "If we confess our sins..." This presupposes that Christians do sin.

Moreover, verse 10 continues the thought, "If we say that we have not sinned, we make Him a liar, and His Word is not in us." Another verse the tape may have used is Numbers 15:30. This verse says that anyone committing a willful sin shall be put to death and that no animal sacrifice is sufficient, and "that person shall be cut off from among his people." This verse does not take into account the myriad number of verses in the New Testament, such as I John 1:9 that says our sins are forgiven in Christ. "If we confess our sins, He is faithful and righteous to forgive us our sins and to cleanse us from all unrighteousness." People also fail to reference Old Testament stories such as that of King David's adultery with Bathsheba. This was a willful sin, yet he was forgiven.

What I took away from the tape, whether or not it was explicitly stated, was that if I sinned even one more time in my entire life, that I would be beyond redemption. In short, it would be the unpardonable sin. The next time I sinned, no matter how minor it may have been... I was guilty! I fell into a deep depression and I felt as if, in the words of a well-known evangelist, I had "out-sinned the grace of God." I thought I had nothing but hell to look forward to when I died, and this life felt so short. What worth would sixty more years in this life be compared to eternity?

I dared not tell anyone of my trepidation and the haphazard church attendance of my mom and I ended shortly thereafter. I had no pastor and there was no mention of God in my home. Furthermore, I had lost the only thing that makes life worth living... hope. In my despair, my weight dropped, and I contemplated suicide. Yet, even that was no escape knowing I only had eternal torment to look forward to... and so, I reluctantly lived in total fear. Feeling that God had forsaken me, I forsook Him. He wasn't very likable anyway... I hated Him! Where was His grace when I needed it most and where was the great comforter in my desperation to do His will?

It was about a year and a half later that I opened the phone book and randomly called a pastor, telling him my problem. He reassured me I had not committed the unforgivable sin and that God would take me back. This could have been a turning point in my life, but it wasn't. Spirituality was not encouraged in my home. In fact, my Dad looked down on Christians and I was still angry at God. Whether I decided for myself, or they decided it for me, I didn't go back.

If I had not lived it, I would find it hard to believe that a sermon tape could derail a person's walk with God for fifteen years, yet that happened to me. Even though I knew the door was open, I didn't go through.

## In the Arms of Other Gods

After much soul searching, I acknowledged I had a "God-shaped hole" within that needed to be filled. I hated the Christian God, so I eventually went looking for acceptance in the arms of other gods. In my late teens, I became interested in the New Age, which ultimately led to my exploring Wicca. I was still searching for truth, love and acceptance from God, but I was looking in all the wrong places.

My first ritual was a Larry Lea binding in San Francisco. Larry Lea was an evangelist who prayed against homosexuality and witchcraft in the city. It was there that I met a girl named Mariah and through her; I got involved in Wicca. The next day was Halloween, and we went to Z Budapest's Halloween ritual. We missed the last bus home and spent the night in the bus terminal. It would be another eight months before I attended another ritual. The day after that Summer Solstice ritual, I got into a disagreement with my parents... and found myself homeless and living on the streets of Berkeley, California for the next year and a half. I attended public rituals because I needed something to believe in during this difficult time in my life.

I found my coven in 1991 by asking for rides home after rituals. I met a couple who lived near my tent and I would stop over to hang out with them on nights they happened to be doing rituals. After the second visit they said they believed it was the goddess's way of saying I should become a part of their circle, and so I did. I was dedicated to the pagan path that same year by them, and in 1992 was initiated as a Witch. I practiced Wicca for approximately five years and began to make a name for myself by attending many public rituals and writing articles for pagan magazines such as Green Egg, Circle Network News, and Hole in the Stone. My first solitary ritual was in 1993 and that was a big step forward for me because it meant that I now had the power in my hands and I didn't have to rely on the high priest and high priestess to do the rites and rituals.

## Mad at God!

I was angry with Christians, no wonder! They followed a God who was mean, vindictive and would smite you for any little thing you did. He demanded more obedience than I could give and I felt that God was disgusted with humanity. When I lived in Berkeley, I used to go over to the university and listen to people taunt the Christian speakers on the plaza. I looked forward to it... involving myself as much as I could. The main reason I wanted to learn about the Bible was to use it as "ammo" against them. Over a period of about eight years, God softened my heart and brought people into my life that have showed me Christian love. By the time I took my second undergraduate course at University I wanted to learn about it for the sake of knowledge, not as a weapon.

## The Beginning of the Beginning

In 1995 I felt compelled to read my Bible, focusing on the New Testament. It didn't seem to do anything at the time except fill some gap. I didn't know why I wanted to read it; I just felt drawn to it.

Then in January 1996, I was leaving for a public Imbolc ritual on the other side of the bay. I was to take the bus to the train, then get picked up from the train station but I never made it. I saw the bus across the street, looked both ways and saw nobody except a car in the middle of the intersection. I made a dash for the bus before it pulled away.

What I didn't know was that behind the car was a motorcycle. He tired of waiting for the car to turn because he was going straight and he hit the gas and zoomed around the car... neither of us saw the other until it was too late. I think he tried to swerve at the last minute, which probably saved my life. I remember seeing the motorcycle speeding towards me and I had enough time to think, "Oh my God, he's going to hit me!" He clipped me with his handlebars and pedal and in that instant, I only saw blackness and felt a searing pain. I cried out to the goddess but received silence. She promised she'd never forsake me... she lied. The next thing I remember my nose was bleeding, and I was sitting barefoot in the middle of the crosswalk.

Someone called 911, and they treated me to the first ambulance ride of my life. They checked me over at the emergency room and I had no broken bones and no internal injuries, just lots of bruises. Needless to say, I didn't make it to the ritual that night.

Salvation begins with God but He often uses people to accomplish His will. In that sense the beginning of the beginning was with Jim, a liberal Christian I had met on the Internet. He went through some difficult times and asked me to pray for him. I began by praying to the goddess whom I worshiped but then thought it best to pray to his God. After all, his request should be brought before his God.

I remember how humbly and apologetically I approached his God that day. I told Him I wasn't asking anything for myself... that I wouldn't expect anything if I did. Then I presented Jim's request before Him. Ironically, I ended up asking for what would be one of the most prophetic things I have ever prayed for. I'm not sure the reason, but twice after my prayer for Jim, I tacked on a request for myself: "God, please help me get to know You." At the time I thought the prayer so trivial that I promptly forgot about it. This only goes to show how important prayer is and that God will hear you as long as you are sincere in your heart, even if you are not a Christian and don't follow Him.

Life seemed to continue on as always but little did I know He was working behind the scenes. It wasn't until shortly after my subtle prayer that I began to see His hand in my life leading me to the next milestone on my journey towards Him.

### Enter Charles

It was February, a month after those prayers, that I met Charles, a Canadian, on the Internet. He became invaluable to me over the next few months, helping to answer my questions and concerns. I believe he was truly sent from God because the timing was impeccable. Charles and I met when I was surfing on the soc.religion.christian newsgroup (an online discussion group). One day I posted these questions: "In one hundred words or less, why are you a Christian instead of something else? Why do you believe? Please, no sermons. I've had quite enough. I just want to know why you believe what you do. Thank you."

As you might imagine I got quite a few responses; some were sermon length and some much more respectful. Charles, being respectful, kept his to 150 words. He gave me a clear, concise answer, but that wasn't what triggered my response. It was a single line at the end of his e-mail, looking more like an afterthought but still an honest question. "Out of curiosity, why are you a pagan?" he asked. And I confidently replied and with that, our correspondence began.

### God Shows Up

One evening at the end of March, I went to a Christian concert held in the gymnasium at St. Mary's College in Moraga. Jesse Manibusan was opening for Margaret Becker and that night

I ditched two pagan events in lieu of this one. I didn't want to admit it even to myself, but I was searching. I have always loved Christian music, and I wanted to buy a tape from Jesse which I could not buy in stores. The show was only $5 and was really nothing spectacular but something happened that I will remember for the rest of my life... I met God. Earlier that evening Jesse played a song called "Open My Eyes." The final verse goes like this, "open my heart Lord, help me to love like you," and I remember sitting there thinking why would anyone want to love like this God? He's so mean! Yet later that night, I felt love. There I was, minding my own business, when I became aware of this incredibly loving presence that filled the room.

After being taught about a God that was mean, angry, and spiteful, this pure LOVE startled me. There was no way to reconcile it with what I had known. I hated God, and had spent the last several years of my life running from Him but even so, He pursued me. His presence dwells in the midst of the praise and love of the people, and there is no doubt in my mind that I was led there to experience it. It took me completely off guard, and when I got home that night and found myself alone in my room, I began to contemplate how some things would have to change. It set me off on a month-long search for this God. It is a scary thing to be chased by God, but exciting, too. You know you're safe and in good hands, but when you're worshiping other gods, you don't know which hands are the good ones anymore. During this time many small coincidences occurred, too many and too small to chronicle here, but more than enough to convince me that this God was real, powerful and that He loved me.

A few days after the concert, I was listening to a secular, lite rock, music station on my Walkman when the song "Right Here Waiting" came on. The chorus goes like this: "Wherever you go, whatever you do, I will be right here waiting for you. Whatever it takes, or how my heart breaks, I will be right here waiting for you." I felt God calling me through that song. It was Him singing... asking me to come to Him.

The following day I heard the beginning of a commercial. I

couldn't tell you what they were selling, but these two sentences leapt out at my ears, "Are you listening? Do you hear it?" That's all I remember, but it was enough to get me to think of God. After all, how does one not listen to God?

Days later, I was captivated by another song on the radio. The chorus went like this: "I loved you, you didn't feel the same. Though we're apart, you're in my heart. Give me one more chance to make it real." In those words I felt God asking me to seek Him one last time before throwing Him away. I felt Him tell me to stop running and just give in and trust.

## Visions and Prayers

There were many times over the month of April that I prayed to Jehovah, asking Him to help me. I reached the point where I told Him that, although I wasn't willing to follow Him, I was willing to become willing. About a week later, I asked Him to help me to love Him.

I desired to know and to learn about Him and prayed that He would show me the way He wanted me to go. I asked for Him to walk with me and tell me how to serve Him. Often I "felt" Him listening and knew I was heard.

I knew that if I was going to get to know this God, I would have to learn to trust Him and so, ironically, I used a technique I'd learned as a Wiccan. Using visualization, I saw myself on one side of a doorway with the goddess standing next to me. Jesus stood on the other side of the open door. I remember saying to Him, "Give me one good reason I should follow You?" His response stopped me in my tracks: "Because I love you." I saw Jesus keep reaching out, telling me to take His hand. Yet no matter how hard I tried... I just couldn't do it.

And then, one night it happened. I closed my eyes to do the visualization, but this time as Jesus reached out, I surprisingly grasped His hand! I knew that He wanted me to step through the door as it was symbolic of real trust, but it took a few more days until I would be ready to take that step. Once I had crossed the threshold, I began trusting God with what little faith I had.

He was patiently working with me to gain greater trust, knowing that I could never ask Jesus into my heart without it.

## Good vs. Evil

While attending college, I found out one of my classmates, named Jay, was a Satanist. One thing I want to clarify is that Satanism should not be confused with Wicca, as Wiccans do not worship Satan, and in fact, do not even believe in him. It is impossible to worship something you do not believe in. Most Wiccans I knew (and still know) are wonderful, law-abiding folks who simply disagree with me in some key theological areas. However, as a Christian I felt that because Wicca does not acknowledge the God of the Bible, it is wrong and therefore evil, though Wiccans themselves are not conscious of this.

Jay and I would occasionally make small talk before class. He was a nice guy who never acted untoward to me, but he freaked me out, anyway. He missed a lot of classes between the beginning of the year and the midterm, but just after midterms he began to show up more frequently. I noticed, instead of sitting in his usual place in the back of class, he was gradually moving forward in the desks until he was sitting right next to me in the front row. Even though he had done nothing to hurt me, his mere presence became a symbol of evil in my life.

I had been thinking about God so much that it overwhelmed my mind, even revealing my fears in symbolic form. It was toward the end of April that I had a dream. It is night and I'm walking toward my college campus. A van pulls up and the Satanist guy from my class is driving. Suddenly, in the way dreams just "move," I'm shocked to find myself in the passenger seat of the van. There is no invitation on his part, and no acceptance on mine. I'm just suddenly there.

I ask him to let me out at the next block, but he is irresponsive... he just keeps driving and soon we are away from the campus area. I frantically crawled behind the front seats to the back of the van, but I soon realize that no matter where I go, I'm still in the van with him. I realize I must get out so I crawl back up front.

I tell him I'm a "white-light, fluffy bunny type Wiccan" and this seems to turn him off.

But the scariest part of the dream was when I asked him, "What do you want?" I will never forget his reply: "To get to know you better." I know it was only my own fears, as good and evil were duking it out over my soul, but it really shook me up. After I had written everything down, it still took me an hour to get back to sleep.

April 1996 was the most difficult month for me with coincidences abounding. I felt God reaching out for me, and yet I kept shrinking back. Due to my interest in Christianity I was attending a class in Christian history at my college. The teacher believed in the hands-on approach and one of our assignments was to go to some services and write a report. We had to attend Orthodox Lenten and Easter services, and a Catholic Easter service. So there I was, struggling with God and required to attend all these services. Don't tell me God doesn't have a sense of humor!

## Acceptance

I realized I was searching for love more than truth, that same love I had experienced at the concert that night. The truth can come later but I yearned so for His love. I told Charles about this and the next day I received an e-mail from him. He wrote, "I see your heart fighting against your will. I have felt God, says your heart, and I want Him. I want to experience that love again. The will responds no, I won't lay aside what I found in Wicca. While the will suppresses the heart, it cannot eradicate the longing. I certainly encourage you to write and speak to Christians about this Jehovah that you do not know but in the end it will come down to the fight between your will and your heart."

Finally, on May 3, 1996 at about 6:45 p.m., I called Charles and had him pray with me, and I gave my life to Christ. But it wasn't during the prayer that I felt it. It was when I said, "I want Jesus in my heart," that I felt I had finally accepted Him. Me, the witch, now a Christian! Ironically, this was four years to the day of my dedication to the pagan path—to the day.

Later I discovered that Charles had experienced a strong feeling he should pray for me that day and that, at the time of my phone call, he had been praying for me, off and on, for about six hours.

### Mysterious Rescuer

About two weeks after my conversion, I had a second dream, markedly different in its mood. I'm at my part-time job in the college cafeteria, just starting my break and am in line at the taco bar to get some food. On the other side of the bar is Jay, also getting some food. He asks me if I would like to go to the movies with him and I tell him, no. Right at that point out of nowhere, a man who I took to be another student, speaks up and tells Jay to lay off me. Jay asks me if he is my boyfriend and I tell him no, wondering myself who he is. Jay and my mysterious "rescuer" exchange a couple more comments I don't catch. At the end, Jay tells my rescuer, "You'd better be careful," and then he goes to sit down to eat. The new guy, my rescuer, just sort of disappears. I couldn't tell you what happened to him but I went to a table furthest away from Jay to eat my food.

Charles said that he believed my "mysterious rescuer" was him because he was praying for me, basically "standing in the gap," and this did not make Satan happy. Perhaps on a subconscious level I knew this and hence had the dream.

### Riding the Fence

Of course, I didn't stop my Wiccan activities right away. Soon after my conversion I attended Ancient Ways, a large pagan festival in Northern California. I felt it may be my last pagan "fling", so I went even though I knew God didn't want me to.

However, I didn't count on Him showing up.

Within one and a half days of arriving I was very confused. I realized later that going there was like walking into a spiritual battle without armor on, like Paul writes of in Ephesians 6. As a new Christian I was a target of the enemy, and here I was willingly walking onto the enemy's ground with no protection! I was so confused that I called Charles all the way in Canada on a pay phone. He told me to talk to God. I said I didn't know if God would listen to me because I was being so bad, but He assured me that God would hear, so I agreed to think about it. Two or three hours later, I went out behind the Meadow Building, sat under the oak tree, and spoke to God... not in prayer, but talking out loud! He heard me and He came.

I hadn't spoken two sentences when I sensed this presence under the tree with me. It took me off guard just like at the concert, but this time, it was personal! He was there because I had called Him. I expected Him to be angry since I knew I was doing something He didn't want me to do, but He wasn't!

But I was angry with His presence because I didn't know what to say and had no desire to repent. I walked off because God was simply being too loving. First, I told Him to get lost but He wouldn't so I finally got up and walked away. I thought if He wouldn't leave, I would. Yet He remained close for the rest of the festival, a constant reminder He was there just waiting for me to call on Him, and to come back. Needless to say, all this made a big impression on me. Later, an acquaintance of mine, Bruce, the man who later baptized me, told me He didn't go away because I had invited Him into my life when I gave myself to Him. He wasn't about to leave me alone. Now I know that He meets each of us right where we are and gives us exactly what we need. I needed understanding and compassion at that point, not judgment, and that's exactly what He gave me.

## Choosing Sides

I was baptized at the end of the summer, but not without a difficult ultimatum. Two days before it was to happen, Bruce discovered that I had not yet renounced paganism. I was still occasionally attending rituals and had no plans to stop. He told me he wouldn't baptize me unless I stopped. It was hard for him to tell me this, and even harder for me to hear it... but it needed to be said. I am glad he put Christ and the gospel before the comfort of either of us. He helped me to understand how important baptism is: How could I undergo a death and rebirth initiation ritual unless I really was dying to my old life? How could I be raised to new life in Christ if I was still holding onto and practicing the old ways?

I mention my baptism because it was an important turning point. I call it my "Joshua moment" because like Israel with Joshua, I was being given a choice of whom to worship. I made the same choice they did, a conscious decision to worship only Jehovah. Giving my life to Him on May 3 was only the beginning, as I had not given up worshiping other gods. He patiently guided me to this decision point.

## Results

Much has changed in my life since I accepted Christ. I have a sense of peace I never had before. Somehow this God puts to rest all the doubts that the goddess never could. Even when I run from Him, I know He still loves me and that someday I will be with Him in paradise. He answers the questions about this life, and the life to come. He tells me everything will be okay, and that He'll never abandon or forsake me. He shows justice tempered with love, which is mercy.

Directly after my conversion my relationship with my boss improved dramatically. Where once he threatened to "let me go" because of my bad attitude, he no longer spoke of this and became downright friendly. My co-workers also mentioned how happy I seemed all the time, and others have noticed my positive disposition saying I complain and worry less. The goddess was not very helpful when I wanted to change these self-destructive behaviors. I was, in fact, unable to change no matter how hard I tried. With God, I didn't have to try... it just happened. The peace and joy He gives really is beyond all understanding, and one's attitude cannot help but change when bathed in this love.

Some people will tell you that Christianity and Wicca can be blended, that you don't have to give up one to practice the other. This is untrue. I tried to blend the two, but at every step the Holy Spirit told me I had to choose (Joshua 24:15).

## If I Could Turn Back Time

How I wish I could go back in time! I would sit down with my ten-year-old self and warn her away from that sermon tape. If she heard it anyway, I would explain the true gospel message of grace, and forgiveness of all sin. I would show her the truth of forgiveness from the Bible.

I remember a picture of me when I was about that age. I am filled with sadness as I look at that little girl and think back on what was yet to come. How I want to fix it and stop the pain!

We live in a fallen world and the god of this world is Satan. He saw a vulnerable little girl interested in the true God and used the legalistic church she attended to draw her away. If it were not for God's direct intervention when I was twenty-five, I never would have found my way back.

## Conclusion

We worship a wonderful God! Who else than the God of the Bible, the only true God, Jehovah, could take an initiated Witch worshiping other gods and bring her to the gospel light? What other god would bother? I deserved justice, and justice dictated that I continue to live - and eventually die - in eternal darkness. But God, in order to show His mercy and magnify His glory, stooped down to me even though I had persecuted Him and blasphemed the very glory I should have worshiped.

I used to worship other gods; now I worship the one true God. Under Joshua's leadership, the Israelites were given a choice of whom to worship: "Choose for yourselves today whom you will serve," (Joshua 24:15). Joshua then told them who he would worship: "As for me and my house, we will serve the Lord," (24:15). And the Israelites chose the same: "Far be it from us that we should forsake the Lord to serve other gods," (24:16). Like Joshua and the Israelites, I too have chosen to follow the Lord and Him alone.

I pray this helps or enlightens you in some way. May God bless you richly as you search for and walk with Him.

# CHAPTER TWELVE

―⚬―

## Taryn Viet

Taryn sought the ways of magick out of revenge and retaliation for the wrongs that had been done to her. Desiring more power, she joined a coven and was initiated into Wicca in South Africa. However, Wicca didn't satisfy her desire, so she pursued the path of high magick and was on the verge of Satanism when she was awestruck by a prophetic word.

It's a flashback in my memory I wish I could forget. I was sitting on the floor crying... terrified while my mother held a gun to my head. This is a bit much for a four-year-old to handle wouldn't you agree? I had absolutely no idea why she was doing this because something inside of me snapped and I could not hear anything except a loud ringing in my ears. It paralyzed me with fear... unable to move because the anger I saw that day was something I have never seen before or again.

This is a part of my life I cannot erase but now I have come to grips with. I recognize that my mother had an emotional problem she could not control. I had to go through a daily process of forgiveness that took years before I was set free.

### Affairs and an Abusive Step-Father

When I was approximately five years old, my father insisted we go to church and all I remember was sitting under his chair and sleeping. My mother, on the other hand, was involved in a satanic coven and my father would later tell me that she dedicated me to Satan while I was still in the womb during one of her rituals. My mother had many affairs, but the breaking point of their marriage was the one with my father's best friend. Beyond being exposed to the painful issues of divorce, my stepfather was an alcoholic who emotionally abused my mother and me. He would hit my mother often and it got so bad that she had to go to the doctor for treatment. Guns, knives and just about anything within reach was involved in his tirades. He threw furniture, broke things, even hit his head against the walls and blasphemed God.

There were times I would hide behind the stove trembling in absolute fear. Besides being his punching bag I also had become his barmaid. I had to pour drinks for him and his drinking buddies, so at nine years old, I started drinking and smoking marijuana from his little outdoor plantation to escape my reality. We hated each other... He tried to strangle me once, and I tried to kill him in his sleep.

### Raped by a School Teacher

Being raped by someone I trusted completely with my life killed a big part inside of me. After the assault, I felt so violated and dirty which affected my soul. I turned to promiscuity to regain control and receive some form of affection in my loveless life. I did not trust men anymore. In fact, I despised them and believed every man I came into contact with wanted to use me, and sex was the only way I could find acceptance. My respect for authority went out the window because he was my authority figure, my schoolteacher. I started to lose my identity at this stage and fell into a deep empty black hole.

My life took a turn for the worse and I strongly needed to find something to stop it from spiraling out of control. Still angry and hurt by my stepfather's rejection, I decided to find a way to kill him without being found out. So, I did research on the occult and practiced "magick" on my own. I went with Wicca because it seemed to be safer and I did not have to be involved in any satanic stuff. I did many spells, all kinds, and most of them worked. The only spells that did not work were the death spells I placed on my stepfather. Unfortunately he was healthy, alive and well. Frustrated, I desired more power, strength and knowledge to get these spells to work. I researched as much as I could and ended up finding the website and address of the coven I would soon join. I contacted them and spoke to the high priestess of the mother coven. This was it! Now I would show the world just how much I hated it.

## Inside the Coven

I arrived for the first time at a Yule festival. The high priest of the coven told me he could sense my fear as I drove up the driveway. The festival started with the normal socializing. Then we went into ritual and as we worked magick, I felt something more powerful than what I did on my own. As the festival ended and it was the time for feasting (a term for eating after ritual to ground), the high priest asked why I was shielding (a process of defense, for protection). I wasn't even aware that I was doing it but because of this he wasn't sure if they could trust me. After attending festivals and being invited to open coven rituals, I eventually dropped my shield and was accepted into the coven. It was required that I attend for a year and a day before they could initiate me into my first degree.

The night of my first degree initiation I felt as though I were poisoned. After drinking from the chalice, it grew hard to breathe and I could barely stand but continued on with the ritual. I felt chilled as the sweat beads poured down my body. There I was, naked, being bound with cords around my ankles, knees and wrists. Something happened, which at the time I could not explain. Halfway through the pathworking (kind of a hypnosis session where you meet the goddess), they gave symbols to me from the goddess. I had to leave the circle as I felt ill and delirious. To this day I cannot remember the oaths I took. A measure, or cord was used to measure my body and then was wrapped around a piece of cardboard, sealed with wax, and signed with my blood in case I caused any harm to the coven. Just after the ritual, two coven members rushed me to the hospital and immediately I was put on an IV drip. The doctor told me I was just about to convulse due to dehydration. I stayed in the hospital for a few hours before being released to return to the coven. I was now an initiated witch.

I was stripped of my old identity and given a new one. I did all I could to please the gods and became infatuated with the high priestess and the elders. Their knowledge was extensive, and I longed to have what they had. I tried bisexuality and had an intense romance with a woman until the relationship ended because deep inside of me; I knew I was not that way inclined.

In time, I got married and had two children. I continued on the Wiccan path. I suspected my husband was having affairs. He drank and was becoming physically violent. Both of us got involved in pornography but only when we were both present. We took drugs together, even during my pregnancies. Only by the grace of God are my children 100% perfect today. One night at 3:00 a.m., I caught my husband on the internet having sexual exploits with another woman behind my back. He threatened to divorce me many times and every time, I would literally grovel at his feet for him not to leave.

## Truth About This Coven

I ended up having a serious love affair with a married man in our coven which lasted a long time. I was in my early twenties at the time and he was fifty-four. I performed many lust and love spells to keep him and later found out that unbeknownst to me; he had done the same. I hated his wife, and she hated the coven, but nonetheless, we continued. We performed many rituals on our own and many of our spells came to fruition. I ended up living in an upper class town with money pouring in and my circle of friends increased. Everything seemed perfect but there would be a price to pay.

Our minds were brainwashed by many pathworkings (hypnosis) in meeting "the goddess". She would direct our paths and rule our lives. During spellworkings, I created a "servitor" or in reality, summoned a demon who would be my spirit guide and servant. Being infatuated by the color blue, I named him Blue. He was gigantic and powerful, with enchanting blue eyes. He donned a long blue cloak and carried a huge staff with a blue crystal on the top. He often spoke to me and told me things about people. He became my best friend. I read people's auras. These, in pagan terms, are the energy fields around a person which determines things about them, also called the spirit-man. During ritual, my coven would often raise energy by drumming. They chose me to enact Persephone, the goddess who descends into the underworld and marries the horned god. There was nothing more fulfilling for me as I felt as though she and I had become one.

I had power now and my spells were working. In the coven we had to study a lot. Most of our time was consumed by classes and they devoted only one third of our time to the ritual itself. We had to read and write reviews for twelve occult books per year. The high priestess led the classes and taught us many things which included Wicca 101, Reiki, chakras, runes and tarot.

They would hold meetings on Saturdays and would end in the early hours of the next morning with partying, sex, drugs and alcohol. This was the highlight of my whole week! If one should fall pregnant during these parties, they would claim the child was a gift from the goddess. Sadly during this time, I had three abortions and three miscarriages. If my husband ever found out, I would have lost him and, though I did not love him, I depended on him for basic needs and finances. One night a few months later he got physically violent with me and I determined I would not be a victim of physical abuse like my mother was, so I finally divorced him.

Around this time, my son had terrible nightmares, and I attributed it to my children's involvement in our coven's rituals. I knew my life was out of control but I just couldn't stop. It was difficult, but I felt it best to give up custody of my children to their father so I would not destroy their lives like I had mine.

## The Gates of Hell

Wicca had become tame, and the married man I was involved with and I went searching for more power, excitement and darkness. He took me to a meeting where many strange people were. Topics discussed were polygamy and the benefits thereof and Gnosis. I realized at this meeting I wanted to be with these people and be involved in "higher magick." After attending a few meetings, they invited us to the "leader's" house.

They took us to the ritual room and upon the altar was a skull of a goat, a chalice which contained blood and various magickal tools. They told us to sit down in a circle and meditate. After about fifteen minutes, a loud bang literally made us jump. They told us that fear raises energy. They explained how different this was from Wicca. The first ritual we would have to attend was called "The Eight Gates," regarding the gates to hell. They would perform this ritual at the next meeting at his house.

They then took us to the front of his house where we were entertained with drinks. He brought out various books of satanic pictures and body mutilations. He then brought out a stack of cards, much like tarot cards only they had sexual perverted images on them. He told us each to take a card, and he read our minds. I asked to see the cards as one would have to look closely at the images to make them out. He then showed us a card of his membership with the OTO (Order of Oriental Templars) which made me very excited. That night, I could not stop thinking about it and couldn't wait until the next meeting.

## Unexpected Prophesy

I had a friend who was spiritual and knew she'd make a great asset to the coven so I went to church with her for no other reason but to show how stupid Christianity was. Once inside, I found I was uncomfortable during praise and worship and I attempted to lip-sync as though I was singing. Finally, the music stopped, and the pastor preached.

As the pastor spoke, it amazed me. He did not stand behind the pulpit repeating religious jargon, claiming to be THE man of God, but he was extremely personable. I was totally shocked when he walked up and down the stage, making hilarious comments. The people laughed often and I couldn't help but feel some kind of release and laugh too. I soaked in everything he said. Then something strange happened. He started to prophesy. I listened to what he said and was totally shocked and somehow, deep inside of me, I knew the words were not from him. They were from this God that they believed in. As the people were encouraged and exhorted with the prophecies, I started to sink lower into my chair. An incredible fear came over me. This love was too much, and I felt unsettled. The next thing I knew, he was right in front of me and I thought, "Just let him say one nasty thing to me and I will curse him." As he spoke, I started to sweat and felt like I wanted the earth to open and swallow me. I was silently screaming, "Get me out of here!"

Then suddenly, I felt calm and could receive what he was saying. "There's a new face here, there's a new face. Yes. You're withdrawn. You are pulled to one side. Like a turtle that pulls into its shell. You build up defense mechanisms, but it's unnecessary. Because yet, you will come to the fullness that God has got for your life. You don't have to hide. Never hide. Step forward. In fact, you came into the church tonight and you enjoyed it very much. You said to yourself you will come back again because you enjoyed yourself. And you were smiling... because something touched your soul. God is saying, "Don't withdraw. Step out because in hiding away, that's where the devil wants you." God wants you because God is saying that you were innocent. You hear what I am saying? You know what I am talking about. God bless you."

I sat back in my chair, half sliding off and felt something I have never felt before. I felt as though my heart had suddenly grown wings and was fluttering. It was the strangest sensation, a wonderful feeling I did not want to stop. I accepted Jesus Christ as my Lord and Savior that night. As I said the sinner's prayer, it felt like light exploded throughout my body. I cried as I realized what was going on and how badly I had been deceived in my past. I felt the love of Jesus come over me and "felt" Him telling me He loves me.

## Breaking Chains

After the service, I left with my friend ecstatically jumping for joy and hugging me. I was so full of energy and could not stop smiling. My new journey had just started when the questions began. What about the coven? What do I do now? One thing I knew I had to do was get my measure back from the coven as that tied me to the occult. I was convinced that they could destroy me with it, so I went back, stole it, then hurried to the church and gave it to them.

The pastor informed me that the demons had come straight for me when they burned my measure at the church. That day, without knowing they were burning it, I crumbled inside. I lost all control of myself and freaked out. My friend was with me and prayed until things were okay.

We had many attacks soon after. One day when leaving church, a sudden heaviness came over us and we kind of freaked. We wanted to go back to the church but God told her to continue straight home. She obeyed and prayed like I have never heard anyone pray before. All I could think was "I will die" while she continued to intercede, then it subsided.

A pastor informed her she must not be afraid because we are surrounded by a legion of angels in the midst of the warfare.

Ironically, soon after, the married man I was involved with had left to go to Europe with his family as his wife got a transfer. We still kept in touch via email. He contacted me one day and told me that he had a feeling I turned to Christianity and if that were the case, he would come back to South Africa and take me back to where I belonged. I tried to explain what an awesome experience I had with Jesus and I tried even harder to convert him as I was naïve and young in the faith. Eventually, I saw a pastor for counseling and he told me to cut all contact with every one of them. How could I possibly do that? I cried many nights struggling to not contact them. They persisted on contacting me and then the threats got so bad; I changed my cell phone number, moved to a different area, cut my long black hair and dyed it.

I became depressed. I felt such sadness, that my friend and I would do spiritual warfare to breakthrough. The journey out has really been tough. Sometimes I wanted to go back to the occult because it was familiar ground. I had many friends there and felt so alone. All I could do was pray and build a relationship with God. Deep down I knew that He was the only one who truly understood.

## Destroying My Occult Possessions

With the help of my friend and her mother, who just so happened to have a ministry for occultists, we put all my magickal belongings in boxes and burned them. While they were burning, I repeated what her mother prayed, and the sparks flew all over, burning my arm. Some objects refused to burn, even books! Something inside of me did not want to burn these items that had taken years to acquire. I had spent thousands of dollars on them and I was extremely attached. As I threw the items in the fire, I cried, questioning if I really had to destroy them but I knew if I were to start my life over, it had to be done. I felt like I was killing my child. I struggled, but had the victory.

When we were done, and we were on our way home, I felt the "energy" again but this time, it was so overwhelming that I fell in love with it. This "energy" was God.

I continued going to church and Christian counseling. My mind was being renewed, but I had a long journey ahead of me and I did not realize it. If I knew then the things I would have to go through, I would have given up and gone back.

## Suicide

I tried to take my life by overdosing on medication on May $4^{th}$, 2005 because I could not handle the pressure anymore. I had no one to speak to who could relate or understand. I was yet, having another identity crisis. My life was spared as my pastor somehow sent me text messages and found out where I lived. I had taken too much medication and the next thing I knew; I was in a hospital, upset that I was still alive. I remember my brother shouting at me and his face distorting out of his hurt, but I could not hear what he was saying. They kept me in the hospital for five days and a psychiatrist diagnosed me with bipolar.

I had to get down on my knees and ask for God's help. I knew I could not do this on my own. Who would think one of the most difficult struggles I would ever encounter in my life–would be my mind?

## The Nightmare

I was wakened some nights in utter fear and I knew this was from the devil. One night after waking from a terrible nightmare, I witnessed one of the most vivid manifestations of my life. I stared at the ceiling while lying in my bed and it began to form somewhat of a circle. It looked like a pregnant stomach... then grew quick and when it came full term; it exploded. The ceiling seemed to have birthed the most hideous creature I had ever seen. I believed it was a demon, and it was looking directly at me! Terrified, I pulled the covers up so that only my eyes stuck out. It swooped straight at me with the most terrible shriek I have ever heard. I yanked the covers straight over my head and broke into a sweat, too afraid to breathe. I just laid there as if I was dead. Eventually, I braved it out to pull the covers down slowly. Nothing was there, but I never slept a second the rest of the night. I prayed instead.

## A Matter of Trust

In the beginning of my walk with God, I could not be around a man who showed any kind of love because I was in bondage to sexual lust. I was also in bondage to drugs, the occult and strangely enough, a craving for blood. I continued these practices for quite some time after I was saved, and each time, I struggled although I was convicted in my heart. Satan kept telling me lies I could escape all my hardships by returning, and sadly, at times, I listened. Until one day, out of fear of God, I fervently prayed and tried to stop. It was then, that God sent my husband to me. I only escaped through Jesus Christ and the help and support of my husband, Richard. Trust. This is something that did not exist in my vocabulary, because of the abuse I had endured throughout my life. I did not even trust myself. Feeling vulnerable, I was paranoid always ready to lash out in self-defense. I shudder to think about the anger I inflicted on my husband.

I had such a severe problem with thinking people wanted to poison me... I could not even trust my husband's cooking. I would say the most vulgar and vicious things, just to hurt him. Now one thing you must know... my husband has the biggest heart I have ever come across and he could not even hurt a fly. At one stage I thought I would break him, but God strengthened him and he continued loving me through it all.

I did not understand love because to me; it was all about lust. I allowed no one close to my heart, and I guarded it with spikes and flaming arrows. I was very hard inside and I used to cry only to manipulate people, but I never cried from my heart. Richard and I would sit on the bed at times and I would just weep because I could no longer contain the pain inside. It was only when I met my husband I was truly able to cry.

I was controlling and demanding, unwilling to submit to anyone. Deep inside I wanted to be in control of my marriage. I knew that if I were to obey God's Word about the woman submitting to her husband; it would be a very long road. After much prayer to God and understanding from my husband, I got to a place where I was willing to submit. I had to have faith because Scripture says, "all things work together for those who love God."

## Promise Keeper

I have accepted that all this has happened for a reason and I can now relate to another person's pain in these areas. I needed a lot of prayer but the journey to full restoration would prove to be a lifelong one. Looking back, I noticed with each passing day, life really gets better and for me it all started when I asked Jesus to be my Lord.

He took me out of the dark hole and lifted me into the light. Suddenly I could see and what I saw was the truth. Since that happened, my life has changed in ways I never could have imagined. Sometimes I feel guilty for all that I have done, but He is a God of restoration which He promised in His Word and He kept His promise, like He always does.

I am happily married with the most caring, loving and supporting man. All my family relationships have been restored and my life is filled with positivity and life. Jesus is now Lord of my life, this transformed my life and saved me from imminent death!

# CHAPTER THIRTEEN

—⚏—

## Ron Harnage

R*on spent twenty-one years determined to prove the existence of the supernatural. In his quest, he delved into many occult practices from becoming an initiated Witch, to exploring Shamanism and Native American Spirituality. He taught witchcraft classes, ran sweat lodges and founded The Coalition of Inter-tribal Native Students but nothing would prepare him for what he was about to witness in of all places, a tent.*

I came to the Lord a little different from most. When I found Jesus, I had been involved in the occult for over twenty-one years. I grew up living with my grandmother who raised me at her home in South Georgia. I had for years disregarded the gospel because I lived a supernatural life and I never saw anything supernatural about the Christians I met. My grandmother would take me to what they call a "hard-shell" Baptist Church. As a child I remember having warm feelings hearing sermons about God's love and I wanted to believe He was for real yet, they had no explanation for what was happening. The home I grew up in was periodically disturbed by what I believed were ghosts or spirits. Pastors and deacons told me this was all a figment of my imagination and that I must be having mental problems... although it seemed like this "thing" would introduce itself to every new house guest. They told me that demons were all in hell since Christ defeated them at the Cross and there are no such things as ghosts, and any sign of paranormal activity was out of the question. I don't recall the pastors or any of the deacons dropping by, though I invited them several times when it was highly active. We left that church when I was about ten years old and went to another Baptist church and at twelve, I was baptized.

My best friend and I, believing there must be more to our spiritual walk, went to Pentecostal meetings and as I recall... I never experienced being born-again. From all outward appearances I did all the Christian things... going to prayer meetings that lasted for hours, some running deep into the night but my personal prayer life seemed dead and the Bible just didn't come alive when I read it. They eventually asked us to leave the Baptist church because the pastor and elders didn't like us going to what they called, "Holy Roller Meetings". Then we went to an Assemblies of God church until my best friend got married and moved away. I found myself alone, cold and disconnected at my new friendless church. About this time I was becoming disenfranchised with Christianity and I started hanging out with my uncle and becoming interested in the occult. I left the organized church because I enjoyed being with my uncle and his friends more than hanging out with some rich, religious elitists. The church acted like they were glad to see me go, though I had been telling them for months I was struggling in my spiritual walk. After that, they used me as a bad example for years and I would hear through the grapevine, "That Ron Harnage guy, he used to come to our church!"

I saw all religion as shallow, weak, and, without believing in the supernatural, they left me with no answers which only drove me to further involvement in the occult.

## My Uncle's Occult Library

Over the years I became familiar with much of the occult world. I spent most of my time investigating and practicing high sorcery. My uncle was into Native American Shamanism, which sparked my interest so I began practicing spirit guide techniques with him. A year later, I was introduced to a sorcerer and demonologist named Randy Simpson and was given access to his occult library. I later learned a lot of the books were rare even in the occult world, let alone in Georgia! With this gold-mine at my disposal, I progressed deeper into the practice of astral projection, meditative states and occult herbalism. None of which really seemed to convince me until I experienced astral travel which solidified the existence of the supernatural.

I learned about summoning spirits from Randy Simpson. I don't recall exactly all that Randy did, but I know he had started out with the Rosicrucians and had left to explore other things. He was pretty much into all the occult, but primarily focused on demonology and working with spirits. I wasn't involved with him for long because I just wasn't interested much in demons and black magick.

In my quest to prove the supernatural, I often performed magickal feats to the skeptics. After going into a trance state, I'd reach into the fire and grab hot coals and squeeze them in my hand without getting burnt or walk barefoot on broken glass without getting cut. If that didn't convince them, I'd use my psychic abilities to tell them secret details of their past. On one occasion, I even amazed my uncle and brother by levitating in the graveyard. These were not magic tricks; they were real supernatural occurrences. Regretfully, I later found such exploits only fueled my brother's interest in the occult which became one of the biggest mistakes of my life.

### Wicca Survival

In my early twenties, I joined Gavin and Yvonne Frost's School of Wicca and completed the initiate's course with them. If you practice what they teach, you'll be a well-trained witch, as this wasn't just some dry correspondence course, but they earnestly took a personal interest in your progress and were open to questions. I communicated with them regularly and they published one of my poems in Survival, their newsletter. Back in the eighties, they made you a first degree if you finished the course, which also included a dedication rite and initiation. They invited me to join their coven, but I remained solitary.

## From High Priest to a Confederacy of Solitaries

I led a small group of students that I taught at home, mostly focusing on trance state meditations and working with spirit guides. Later I briefly became the high priest of the Circle of Artemis, in Athens, Georgia around 1992-93. The high priestess had come from one of Ray Buckland's covens and it was basically Alexandrian Wicca. I was primarily solitary, but I was always hanging out with other witches, in an uncoven confederacy of solitaries, if you will. One night a young witch came to me for help because she had gotten herself in trouble with some Satanists. This opened a door for me to become involved in helping people who felt they were being victimized by Satanists or who had lost a loved one through them. I even helped someone leave a satanic coven.

About a year later I helped two friends who had come out of Ray Buckland's second coven, to run Mother Earth Books and Herbs in Athens where we held meditation and yoga sessions. Two years later, the local churches ganged up on us and had the city shut us down. During this time I became involved with the Atlanta Area Rainbow Family.

I helped lead ceremonies with the Rainbow Family of Living Light, including handfastings and occasionally sweat lodge ceremonies. They split this group into regional "families" that operate like a coven but in a looser sense. I taught guided meditation, working with spirit guides, psychic self-defense and had healed people of leukemia and cancer with occult herbalism.

## Tribal Shamanism

In 1997 I met Dr. Lee Francis, a Native American from the Laguna Pueblo tribe. He had been involved with the Edgar Cayce Foundation and had also authored a book on emphatic abilities. We became close friends while his career was shifting from teaching at the University of Missouri to the University of New Mexico. He invited me to come and join his staff at the Native America Studies Department. I accepted a position sponsored by his organization, the Wordcraft Circle of Native American

Writers and Storytellers. While I was there I worked as a human rights activist and founded the Coalition of Inter-tribal Native Students. We held the first Native protest since 1972 to stop the university from closing down the Native American Studies Department. It was a three-day prayer vigil that gained national attention. We also hosted tribal shamans from all over the west.

## Moral Convictions

The whole last year before I found Jesus was just insane. Everything was falling apart with one disaster after another. During this time, I was preparing to open a New Age school but when I would do my daily meditations and creative visualizations to help me focus on bringing it into being; visualizing myself doing lectures would suddenly change to my standing behind a pulpit preaching. I didn't even know Scripture much less believe in it which was very disturbing to me. It eventually got to where I quit meditating because it kept happening. Well, that didn't help because I heard this "inner" voice with a long message that went something like, "You shall return unto the God of your fathers, and I will restore your soul and heal your spirit. I will give you a place with honor in my kingdom and wipe away your shame, and I shall give you power to proclaim my kingdom," God of my fathers, how could this be when my dad was an atheist?

My girlfriend who was also a witch, and who came from a family of witches, started to sense something in her spirit and went to her uncle who is a seer. Strangely, she came back telling me he saw I would become a Christian which started her teasing, calling me, "church boy."

Desperate for answers, we went to a Hastings bookstore because I was hunting for every book on divination I could find as I couldn't meditate and my psychic powers seemed to be totally drained. It was crowded, so I sat in the back where it was quiet. I was reading some New Age books that was in the Christian section. She came back and spotted me, "Oh I see! You're sitting right at home."

"What?" I said, as she pointed to the sign overhead that read,

"Christian Literature." Then she vehemently added, "I just saw it. My uncle is right; you will become one. You will become a preacher!" This only confirmed the message I received using divination which was that I would spend the rest of my life working on my moral convictions.

So after years of work, I took some time off to go home and visit my parents. My mother was saved three years prior and became a Pentecostal Sunday school teacher. Even though I was heavily involved in the occult, I didn't have any problem with this. I wasn't a Satanist and was basically a peace-loving person who wasn't prejudiced toward people, even Christians. I felt it was fine if it made my mother happy, but it just wasn't for me.

## What about Jesus?

I did however, as misguided as I was, talk to God often. He had been pursuing me for years but unfortunately I didn't listen to Him much, although I could still hear Him. I remember distinctly on one occasion He asked me, "Have you considered my Son Jesus?" I replied by telling Him I didn't mind Jesus at all, but it was His people I had problems with. I continued with this mindset for the longest time.

I know now that the devil consistently sent religious people into my life to reinforce my belief that Christianity was for shallow people and that there was nothing supernatural about it, but things were about to change.

## Jesus Loves You

A Pentecostal tent revival came to town while I was visiting my mom in Lake City, Florida. It was Pastor Tommy Drumm and my mother was all worked up wanting to go, insisting my stepfather and I go too. She was persistent and I think the only reason we finally agreed to go was so she would leave us alone. We went opening night and once we got there, there was a lot of singing and praying. The pastor began to preach and I think my mind wandered off somewhere, but the next thing I knew he had called someone up to pray over them for healing. This really got my attention. I was curious to see what would happen next especially because I was a white witch, meaning I used witchcraft and medicinal herbs to cure people.

He prayed over a lady that had come forward who had cancer. He fervently prayed for her and she began to jump up and down, shouting that she was healed and praising God. I was thinking this has to be a fake and maybe he just paid her to do that. I knew it took me several days to heal someone with cancer. He kept calling more and more people up and I continued seeing the same results... excited people saying they were healed and praising God. I came back night after night because I had to figure this thing out!

Something was going on! God had caught my attention! After a few nights it became obvious it was no con game. I was perplexed, "No one could afford to pay all those people to act like they were getting healed."

So, I began to take an interest in what he was preaching. Although God's supernatural power got my attention, it was the preaching on the love of Christ (and not damnation), which began to change my heart and mind.

Preaching on hell wouldn't have done me any good. I had heard all about it before. I wasn't scared of it or its demons as I had lived with that almost all of my life. But hearing that God really loved me and that He sent His only Son to demonstrate His love for us, now that was something almost too good to be true!

So one night, I came home from the tent revival and I was looking through the Bible in my room. I was laying there and read the book of Matthew. I really wasn't sure about this Jesus guy yet. I considered myself a man of peace and the occult had taught me some liberal ideas about love and tolerance (the law of karma), and some things Jesus had to say just didn't sit right with my ideology. I thought I should bring this up because I see so much of the same thinking in the Church. The Bible should be followed, not the law of karma; however, that was a digression.

I hadn't made my mind up yet, but I was finished reading for the night, so I turned my light off and went to bed. I was laying there in the dark trying to sleep when I heard the closet door mysteriously open, then the lamp next to my bed suddenly crashed to the floor and the blinds beat against the window.

I knew what it was... it was a demon trying to scare me. I was lying there indecisive what to do next. I really did not like demons and I concluded that if they did not like what I was considering, then it must really be a good idea!

### The Holy Bible?

Frustrated, I got up and flipped the light switch on the wall and skimmed through the Bible. The activity did not cease but became more dramatic. The closet door was opening and closing, the window blinds continued banging and now I heard scratching and hissing.

I was panicking but I remember from believers who had witnessed to me before that there was some type of prayer of salvation. I hurriedly flipped through the pages to find it and after a couple minutes I became even more frustrated.

"It's too big of a book!" I thought to myself.

I had no idea where it was, and of course like any skilled witch, I knew it had to be done the right way, with the right spell. I also knew though, that sometimes with the supernatural you just had to improvise.

So I gave up trying to find it in the big book and in desperation called on the Lord. I asked Him to save me and forgive my sins. I told Him I believed He had raised His Son from the dead. I asked Jesus to be my Savior and Lord, and from that night forward I was a changed man!

The next night I returned to the revival and publicly confessed Jesus as my Savior and Lord. I was baptized in the Holy Ghost and felt the entire world lift from off my shoulders as I felt the spirit of God come in. The activity stopped that night, but shortly after, strangely returned. I kept wondering why it didn't cease and asked God about it in prayer and he directed me to Scripture about cursed objects. I was a little reluctant to get rid of my occult paraphernalia because some items had sentimental value and some things were quite rare so I thought I could at least sell them. I distinctly remember that evening was the night before trash pickup, so I took everything which I already had placed in a box and took it outside to the curb.

The activity still didn't stop and this whole thing was driving me crazy. Then a few nights later I was standing in my bedroom praying and I asked God why it hadn't stopped. Suddenly, the closet door popped open and that same box was sitting there! So this time I took it out to the woods and burnt everything. Things quieted down as far as the paranormal activity goes but the enemy was still heavily attacking me.

I experienced oppressive attacks from what seemed a multitude of demons using doubt as their main weapon to question my salvation. I heard their voices, from the time I would wake up in the morning to the middle of the night. At first I'd hear God's still small voice encouraging me, then shortly after I would hear demonic voices saying, "You're not saved... witches can't be saved!" I was experiencing heaven and hell at the same time but to me the most terrifying threat was, "We have you on our list and we are expecting you down here... you're not getting away from us!"

It was several weeks before I believed without a doubt that I was saved. The enemy put up quite a fight because he hates seeing a lost soul get saved, let alone, one of his own servants! As the days progressed, and the attacks continued, the Lord led me to an occult object that I had long since forgotten.

You see... my beloved brother Brian, had become a Satanist years before his death, although I tried my best to dissuade him. I had just finished praying and was going to the kitchen to get something to drink. As I passed by the window, my parent's storage shed suddenly loomed at me in hyper-focus. I asked the Lord about it and He seemed to be directing me to go out there. He told me that there was something that had belonged to my brother he wanted me to get rid of.

I went out to the shed, feeling a little apprehensive, but I knew I was being led by the spirit. It was one of those big wooden sheds with a lot of storage and as I entered; I heard the Lord tell me to look in the attic. I thought to myself, "Oh boy... it would have to be all the way up there!"

As I was walking towards the ladder that led up to the attic, the garden rake mysteriously came off the wall just like someone had picked it up and was swinging it at me! It came right directly to the front of my face and then stopped like it had hit an invisible wall... then fell to the floor, lifeless. As I was trying to emotionally regroup and digest what had just happened, a large push broom stopped just short of smacking me in the face, before falling to the floor as well!

I scurried up the ladder and found a bunch of boxes but the Lord knew which one contained my brother's belongings. He directed me right where to look as though I'd been there before. I found it there in the box and I knew as soon as I saw it. It was a black piece of marble from a cemetery that my brother had used for scrying. It brought back all the suppressed memories of the day he had come home with it years before. I took it outside and smashed it to pieces with a hammer and threw it away. After that, these horrendous attacks on my life calmed down.

I wanted to share this with you just to show how bad it can be if you have unclean things in your possession. This will give the enemy a territorial claim on your property. It opens a gate to the demonic and can wreak havoc in your life. I believe it is the reason that some of us have the problems that we do and also the reason that some of us are sick.

Deuteronomy 18:10–"There shall not be found among you anyone that maketh his son or daughter to passeth through the fire, or that useth divination, or an observer of times, or an enchanter or a witch, or a charmer, or a consulter with familiar spirits, or a wizard or a necromancer." This includes some things Christians seem to think are harmless like zodiac symbols, horoscopes, tarot cards, Ouija boards and even watching psychics on television. These things may seem entertaining and fun, but I assure you they are not. You can open yourself up to spiritual influences you really don't want operating in your life. Take it from me... someone who knows.

I really had to struggle to get out from under it, but all that fighting taught me how to pray and seek His presence! Glory to God for coming into my life and I thank Him daily for rescuing me from something that few people break free from and now I find joy in helping others, ministering to all walks of life; but I have also been used by the Lord to lead many out of witchcraft, so many that I have lost count.

It gives me special joy to lead a lost soul to the Lord, but even more so a witch, because I know how deceptive it is and how few escape.

## Blood Bought

I believe this all came about because I had a praying mother. I see so many Christian parents that have just given up on their children because they are so far gone, but I believe I am living proof that you're never too far that God cannot get a hold of you. I also think on that Great Day there will be a lot of praying parents up in the front of the line!

Are you a witch? Do still practice the occult? Do you think you are doomed for hell? Or are you just a sinner?

I have GREAT news for you today! Today is your day of salvation. There is only ONE way out of hell, satanic practice, vows, oaths or your sin–The Blood of Christ!

Pray this simple prayer now:

Lord Jesus, I know I'm a sinner and I am sorry for my sins, please forgive me and come into my life. Be my Savior and my Lord from today on. I reject the kingdom of darkness and all it stands for; I reject and denounce the lordship of the devil over me. Devil, you are not my master any more, from this moment I have nothing in common with you again. I choose the path of life found in Christ Jesus who loved me and gave Himself for me.

I am now washed and cleansed completely by His Blood that was shed for me on the Cross. I ask that God will put the mark of Christ on me with His indwelling Spirit because I am His and He is mine. Thank you, Jesus! Amen.

# CHAPTER FOURTEEN

## Shalom Shick

Shalom had been a practicing witch for over twenty years, studying at the Ravenwood Church and School of Wicca and well connected in the pagan community. A onetime representative of the Witches' League for Public Awareness and ordained by the Church of All Worlds, Shalom belligerently confronted the Prince of peace never expecting what would happen next.

Remember the last excellent movie you went to? It gave you such a remarkable experience that you wanted to share it with everyone and especially the people you care about. But you knew your best friend didn't like mushy romances, so you were reluctant to tell her about it and yet you were certain that if she saw this romance film, she would love it. Now add to that the fact that this film was actually so powerful that it turned your whole world upside down, changed your entire perspective on life and made everything so much better, even to the point of saving your life! Now you are not only motivated by the desire to communicate your experience, you want your friend to have the chance to change her life too, and find solutions to those life problems just as you did.

Some time ago, I used to tell people, "I know Christians who witness and mean well, but I just don't need to be saved from anything. I don't buy into all that 'hell-fire-and-damnation' stuff like they do. They think I worship Satan, when they spend a lot more time on him than I do! I don't even believe in Satan at all!" Well, guess what? I now know that Satan is for real, and to avoid his traps we had best know that, and I did need saving and in a big way as I was drinking, drugging, sleazing, trash talking and unhappy.

I was a goddess who was failing miserably, having had three abortions, four failed marriages, tried lesbianism and ménage à trois, and been a burglar, shoplifter, drug dealer, hooker and topless dancer. I was a practicing witch and had been for over twenty years, but my magick wasn't helping me when I felt that I needed it most. I had studied the religious philosophies of Deepak Chopra, Louise Hay, Marianne Williamson, Course in Miracles, and many others all in the search of truth, and I thought I had a good handle on it.

## Before Salvation: The Witch

I was raised with a liberal Christian upbringing. I went with my mom to Methodist and Presbyterian churches now and then, primarily for Christmas and Easter. I grew up without a father, and that has colored my ability to relate to Abba Father from the outset. I don't think many people realize how critical the traditional family unit with a mother and father role model really is for children being able to grow up spiritually and emotionally strong. At home, my mom often read palms and did tarot for friends and my grandmother read our astrology signs daily so these were some early influences that the enemy used to draw me away from the truth I was really seeking.

As a teenager I had a bad church experience just after believing I had received "salvation," having been led by a girl to say 'the sinner's prayer.' I was so excited; I went with her to their church service the very next night to get baptized. I had never had a full immersion baptism, only the Methodist 'sprinkling,' and thought it sounded like a great idea so I brought my towel and a change of clothes. After the service she had me talk with the 'elder' and he said, "I understand you've given your heart to Jesus and you'd like to be baptized?"

"Yes, sir!" I happily replied.

He then asked, "Have you received the gift of tongues?"

I enthusiastically answered, "No, but I'm fervently praying for it and I know it will come."

His reply infuriated me, "Well we can't baptize you."

I was outraged and hurt, immediately lashing back, "Then I'm outta here!" I cursed at him, then declared, "I've been reading a lot about witchcraft and it makes way more sense to me than this!" and with that I took off vowing never to set foot in another church and I didn't, with only a couple of rare exceptions on one holiday and a few weddings, for over twenty years.

## Ravenwood School of Wicca

Shortly after that, the enemy was very accommodating to provide an open door for me to join the first public coven in the country, Ravenwood Church and School of Wicca, which at the time in the late 1970s, was in Atlanta. I went there to study Wicca for a while and ended up moving in with a high priest and high priestess who were highly touted at Ravenwood and the entire Wiccan community, who had their covenstead in Chattanooga. I studied under some great names in Wicca, one of the most notable being Sybil Leek; who was involved in repealing the witchcraft laws in England years ago. At the time, I thought it was "way cool" to have hobnobbed with all these renowned Wiccans, because I could readily name drop my way into high regard with new Wiccan friends and covens.

I really believed I was becoming more enlightened and was being led to the truth. It was a beautiful religion, with a beautiful philosophy... worshiping nature, dancing in the moonlight naked and all kinds of "fun" stuff. This "fun" included attending raucous pagan gatherings that were nearly always saturated in drugs and alcohol and orgies.

I continued practicing for over twenty years, primarily as a Solitary Witch, though for a number of years, I camped out for days at a time at a well-known group of covensteads that were located adjacent to one another creating a kind of community in Cosby, Tennessee for solstices and equinoxes. There were four hundred attendees from all over the country at many of these events and, if only folks knew just how many covens are nearby, even right here in the Bible belt, I think they'd be mightily surprised.

I believe that the prayers of my mother and grandmother, backslidden though they were, kept me from many things that could have proven to be the end for me. It is interesting that I never followed through with initiation, although my high priest and high priestess stated that I really didn't need to as they would always vouch for my standing in the pagan community and they are still held in high esteem among Wiccans, so their word was greatly respected. I was even appointed to be the first Tennessee state representative in the Witches' League for Public Awareness, a kind of PR group for 'the cause' of Wicca. We had a clean-up mile on a local road with a sign marking our area which is still there to this day.

The Church of All Worlds ordained me to perform handfastings, which are like a wedding and did so frequently, one of which was for a lesbian couple, though we didn't file it with the local courthouse.

### Cat Out of the Bag

I didn't believe in sin, which opens the door for just about anything you want to do. Even though I practiced magick and attended pagan gatherings, I kept having terrible experiences and my life was getting worse, yet I thought I was growing spiritually. Still, things kept going wrong in my life and I found my magick and philosophy didn't help, nor did the gods and goddesses.

When I was twenty-five years old I was engaged to marry a fellow, I was really nuts about. My high priest and high priestess were going to perform the ceremony in Raccoon Mountain Cavern in Chattanooga, and it was going to be the first wedding ever there. The Chattanooga Free Press was coming to cover the wedding and yet we were doing it under cover, so that our friends and relatives wouldn't easily guess that it was really a Wiccan handfasting.

We were all camping out in the valley there the night before the wedding, having a big party, with lots of inebriating party supplies for everyone until the cat was let out of the bag as my fiancé's brother's wife took his folks aside and told them that she knew from watching the 700 Club what the funny stars we were all wearing stood for: we were witches! They got together and did a prayer circle around him, finally convincing him to leave that very night... I was devastated. They wouldn't let me talk to him after that and he never had anything to do with me again. I will never forget that pain and I turned to my magick hoping to find peace. I thought it was because I wasn't in harmony with nature enough so I spent time worshiping my favorite tree, casting spells and searching for answers from the god and goddess.

### Prince Charming?

Many years later, I stopped by a bar and met a charming fellow named Kevin. Before long, we had fallen in love and decided to marry. I also adored his two daughters, Brittany and Brooke, almost as much as him. Once again, his Christian family found out I was a witch and convinced him that he and the girls were in spiritual danger by having me in their lives and they were. I had already taught the children banishing spells and how to invoke using the sign of the pentacle. I was absolutely crushed having lost not only him but his children. So after trying all kinds of magickal spells and meditations and exhortations to all the gods and goddesses I could think of, I finally decided that who I needed to be talking to was Jesus, since this was all His people's fault. So I had a hard and vicious talk with Him peppered generously with profanity, letting Him know that if He was going to encourage stuff like this, He'd better do something about the consequences.

### Encountering the Prince of Peace

I told Him, "They say you are the Prince of peace, well I need some peace here." I was having this little chit-chat with him because I never doubted that He existed but rather believed that we were all sons and daughters of God and he wasn't special in any way. I wanted relief from this deep horrid pain of loss and abandonment I felt to the marrow of my bones so I finally broke down and began to beg for it. What was really strange was I did feel this incredible wave of peace, relief and hope? The power that I felt at the time was phenomenal and I realized that there was a power in this whole philosophy and that it wasn't just a religion for people who needed someone to tell them what to do which is what I had always thought. There was something to this Messiah after all.

Over time, more miracles manifested as God was showing me His face after all these years of seeking Him in all the wrong places. I began to research this religion that I had thought of as being for sheep-like, unintelligent people for so long. I read some apologetics literature, most notably Lee Strobel's "The Case for Christ" and "The Case for Faith," which were very compelling. As you may know he began as a journalist to debunk Christianity and just like my experience, the more he dug, the closer he got to God. I soon realized that Christianity was a very intelligent religion based on solid facts contrary to my former viewpoint of Christians as stupid people who couldn't think for themselves and I soon found that no other religion had so much history and archaeology to back it up. No other religion had a God that had given them step-by-step instructions on how life could be so much better and I saw how compassionate it was for Him to give us His Word and promises in the Bible.

I started to experience the veil-like scales being lifted from my eyes as Scripture tells us that often we do not see truth because the enemy deceives us by obscuring our vision. When we allow the Holy Spirit to take up residence within us, this is removed and things we once thought foolish are seen in their true guise as wisdom... a fascinating phenomenon!

### Becoming Shalom

Seeing that I was now seeking God the Father, Kevin came back into my life and we read the Bible together and going to church. I struggled with much of what the church said, but as I studied and began to read Scripture, more and more was being revealed. At this time, we were still partying but then, a very significant miracle took place. It was Thanksgiving, 2001 in Knoxville, and I dropped by Rookies, a sports bar to watch the University of Tennessee game on their big screen and soak up a couple of pitchers of suds. That was nothing to me back then, as I had quite the tolerance built up for alcohol, particularly beer but something happened that is difficult to describe. After I left the bar and got home, I had an unusually intense panic attack. I became incredibly afraid and felt as though I was going insane or that I would die. The next day, I realized something peculiar had happened as I was paranoid of getting intoxicated again. I fell off the wagon only five times over the next year but never over the top, which I believe is miraculous considering the prior twenty-seven years of my carefree, partying lifestyle.

I got baptized and joined Calvary Baptist Church on April 14, 2002 and married shortly after. I always wanted Yahweh's peace; His shalom in my life and it was one of my challenges to be serene. My old names both had distinct pagan origins, unbeknownst to my mother. As a Wiccan I had been proud of them but I decided I wanted to make the same change that Abraham, Peter and others had made. I went right down to the courthouse where I shared my testimony with others as I shared my purpose for changing my name.

## Hebraic Roots

My first Hebraic Roots experience was at a Messianic Congregation in Knoxville, which is comprised of both Jewish and non-Jewish believers in Yahshua (aka, "Jesus"), usually with Jewish leadership. I seem to be one of the few who has been brought to the Hebrew Roots of our faith, and it has brought me so much closer to Him even than when I was first born-again! It is such a rich connection to follow our Savior in the footsteps that He walked, worshiping in the ways He worshiped, keeping His Shabbats and Appointed Times, looking forward to His soon glorious appearing.

Yom Kippur and Sukkot were great! I put my air mattress and

sleeping bag out on the roof of the apartment just outside my bedroom window for a little Sukkah. It got too cold the first few nights though, and I had to wimp out. But the nights that I was able to sleep and eat out there were so special. I really felt like maybe I was making Abba smile at my little gesture and it also gave me a chance to talk to a few folks about what I was doing, so witnessing ensued as a result too. Little did I know that when I changed my name to 'Shalom' I had created an opportunity for a funny inside joke upon going to the Messianic Congregation. Several people, especially our congregation leader, enjoy greeting me with: 'Shalom, Shalom!' which really tickles me.

## After Salvation: The Saint

My faith was put to the test when my seven-year marriage shockingly ended. I felt betrayed as divorce was the furthest thing from my mind. I felt helpless and angry in the position I now found myself as my emotional and spiritual bonds with this man were being severed against my will. I had strong convictions for the sanctity of marriage and took my vows seriously, so this breach in our marital commitment was overwhelmingly painful. The next couple of years I searched the Scriptures as I struggled with so many unanswered questions. Here, I had thought my life was finally on track and I believed I was walking according to Yahweh's plan only to be alone and heartbroken. Despite what could have devastated me, I found I was not walking this road of despair alone, rather Yahshua and I walked hand in hand. He more than anyone, understood my betrayal and abandonment on a personal level and He was my comfort in my time of need. I'm not saying the road has been without suffering by any means, but by putting my trust in Him alone, I've gained a bond that is stronger than death and an unconditional love no fellow could match.

With the trauma of the divorce behind me, my road to recovery began. For the first time it was just Yahshua and me. Ironically, the very relationship that had sent me calling for help to Yahshua while I was a witch also sent me helplessly crying at His feet now. The perfect little fairy tale in life one hopes for, reconciliation and riding off into the sunset didn't happen.

It is very important that believers understand that following Yahshua is not going to make your life easier. It may make it more difficult yet one must always keep in mind that what is right and true is always more of a challenge, but definitely worthwhile. Yahweh will give you the means to make it through even with the pain and rejection that are likely to result. We must not be like those evangelists who try to convince everyone that being a believer will make everything rosy. For it is those who the enemy loves to use to keep us from realizing the truth ahead of time so that we won't be so disappointed when it doesn't turn out the way we were deceived into believing and then fall away like the parable of the sower and the thorns. (Matthew 13:1-9)

## In Retrospect

I now realize that the labyrinthine path I took to Yahweh resulted from very poor decisions on my family's part and my own. I can see where things could have been different if I had known and studied Yahweh's Word in the Scriptures but He did patiently use that path to finally reveal Himself to me and He continues to do so day by day, Hallelujah! I also realize that the path through Wicca allows me to have experienced what few believers possess, so that there is an audience that needs to hear the things that I can speak to and plant seeds within, and that is what I believe is behind all of us who used to walk that twisted path. Now I no longer seek to educate the world on who witches really are, but on who Messiah is. I just want folks to know that Yahshua truly changed my life. It may not happen like a lightning strike but as a step-by-step process, like it was for me. He can be so very gentle. Talk to Him today and let Him move in your life. Just try it and see... you won't be disappointed.

# FROM THE CRAFT TO CHRIST

# CHAPTER FIFTEEN

―∽―

# Mark Bishop

*Mark was a perceptive child whose spiritual journey began with parapsychology studies and psychic development. He engaged in various magickal practices ultimately transforming from magician to a Solitary Eclectic Witch until he discovered those whose lives were truly a living testament.*

It all started when I was a child... I could occasionally see and hear creatures that people around me apparently could not. I could also visualize and feel energy patterns, like fine glowing threads around me.

As I grew older, I discovered that I could momentarily foresee into the future with incredible accuracy. During the soda promotions, I knew which bottles had the winning caps and I could always pick winning numbers for door prizes, not only for myself but also my friends. I even envisioned my future tennis instructor; these were just a few examples of this inherent gift.

My initial attraction to witchcraft in its many forms was that it seemed to provide answers for the things I was experiencing in my life, and the abilities I possessed. I started my spiritual journey with psychic studies and parapsychology, and then took detours through various magickal paths to see what 'worked'.

## Shipwrecked Salvation

When I was twenty-one, I heard the gospel for the first time in a friend's apartment. He told me that Jesus died for me and offered me His salvation. At the time, he had no idea what I was into so we spoke at length that afternoon and to my surprise, I accepted Jesus that very day.

The next few months were good ones, as I read the Word and prayed... until I entered the military and was shipped off to basic training, which is where I found a serious concentration of bunk in the 'Name of Jesus'. Unfortunately, my newfound faith shipwrecked later that year on the shoals of what I saw from some church folks that I ran across after enlisting.

These sailors were simply exploiting their Sunday morning 'prayer time' just to dodge the Company Commander. When you combined that with the barefaced callousness of the military Chaplain, it was a recipe for disaster. I reasoned, if they were the end result of being part of the church, I'd much rather go back to magick and that is what I did, walking away from my Savior and deeper into the shadows than before. Looking back, that was a rather short-sighted and foolish decision, but it was my choice, none the less.

## On the Waterfront

One dark night on the waterfront, I was confronted by an entity that had decided my will had been 'free' long enough. What ensued was a battle of wills, with it attempting a possession with the proper 'bait'. The offer was power... lots of it and I almost lost myself that night, for it got inside my defenses. It did something that made me furious. As dawn approached many hours later, I finally was able to use the power of that rage, to break free but I still bore the scars on my soul from that black night.

In hindsight, I have to wonder if I had truly broken free or if it had succeeded in its diabolical plan after all, as lying dormant, deep beneath the surface. This entrenched rage had its grip and over the years has created a great hindrance in my life.

After that scare, I started a new path... new for me anyway. I experimented, mostly focusing on magick in a more serious way and with a little guidance along the way, I transformed from magician to witch. I was trying to uncover the Old Ways, not Wicca per se... although I incorporated some of those practices. This curiosity and practicality led me on the path in what I can describe as a Solitary Eclectic Witch, with a loose definition; borrowing things from different paths rather than choosing only one. I pulled from Shamanism, psychic, and a Celtic variant of witchcraft. As with everything, I followed my instincts as I blended them all together. While I had some friends who were involved in their own occult explorations, I would forgo covens in favor of working solitary. There was a multiplicity of reasons for this, including it being easier to focus on one's own will rather than several and I didn't believe in having 'help'... choosing instead in being my own council.

## The Eye of the Storm

Later on, an issue came up with the 'gods' I followed and I abandoned them after a disagreement over a matter that was incredibly important to me, but not to them. I tried to magickally intervene with a North Atlantic storm without their help or permission, but my attempt failed and the ship I was trying to help tragically went down. Since I had severed all ties with them, I went back to searching for what I thought was truth. That search took me further into magick for about another year while I resisted the call of Jesus to come back to Him.

A transfer and various circumstances led me to a Christian Serviceman's Center that had an inordinate amount of occultists hanging around. Since I was comfortable on both sides of the spiritual fence, I saw this as an excellent opportunity to get off the base. At the request of the Center's director, I attended different churches with the Sunday crowd.

## Living Testimonies

I discovered little congregations with big hearts and Christians that were trying to follow Jesus, actually desiring to live out their faith. Of course, I also visited a couple churches that had me wondering if we were talking about the same Jesus. It was during this time I was drawn back to The Lord as these true followers of Jesus were like living testimonies giving me something to seriously contemplate in my quest for answers.

Initially, I was not planning on giving up magick, rather placing that ability under God's control and authority while pursuing the path of a Christian magician... what was I thinking?

I know that will be a foreign concept to many of you but there are those who turn to Jesus for salvation but continue with magick as before... either not calling upon other deities or rather giving Jesus top billing, attempting to keep a foot in both worlds. This is due in my estimation to a serious lack of understanding of both what it means to follow Jesus, and how things in the supernatural realm actually work. The Lord convinced me that this was the wrong way to go about doing things and a choice had to be made. Having been wired in such a way that magick became second nature, laying it aside would prove to be no easy task.

## April Fool's Day

While this decision was extremely unsettling, it allowed me to give an honest answer when my bride-to-be, asked if I was done with magick. Finally, I had enough but as I had long since progressed beyond the need for much in the way of 'tools,' removing the magick that had so entwined my life for years would be quite the challenge. Occasionally I would fall under its temptation until that one spring morning, April Fool's Day (how appropriate) I awoke feeling like a great weight has been lifted from me... I just knew I was free and the battle was over!

After I returned from duty, I uncovered some of my old books on magick and threw them away. Within a couple of days, one of them mysteriously showed back up again, so this time I decided to burn it. Incredibly, even after dousing it in lighter fluid... it would not ignite until I prayed over it and the fire consumed it. Over time, I destroyed a couple of my staffs and tossed a ring that I had used to store energy in case the need arose. Instead of just asking God to cleanse them so I could keep them, I felt it was His will for me to make a clean break and remove them from my life.

## John 3:16

Over the years, I have learned much. Some of those lessons were that there are no perfect cookie-cutter Christians which is great news since I don't seem to fit that mold very well. I have also learned that there are still some church folk who think that magick and witches don't really exist and others who think that witches can't be saved. Of course, since they think I can't be saved and truly follow Jesus, that must mean my only reason for being there is to corrupt the Church.

Don't get me wrong, many are well meaning believers trying hard to follow Jesus, but they have been led astray from the biblical truths. In fact, when talking with some of them, it merely takes pointing out the applicable Scriptures such as John 3:16 to get them to understand and rejoice that even witches can be saved.

Usually when you point them back to that familiar verse, they gain the revelation that nowhere does it say that it is easy to introduce an occultist to Jesus, but that His offer of salvation applies to them as well, if they will accept Him.

## ExWitch Forum

Since coming back to Jesus in 1989, He has used my life in many ways... from Sunday school teacher to song leader, from choir to the orchestra. I passed out gospel tracts in Texas, took part in a prayer walk in Illinois, shared in a theological debate on various forums and ultimately reached out to the occultists of the world with Jesus' love.

During my years with the ExWitch web forum, we shared the gospel with many and encouraged those seeking answers. We never watered down the gospel but we presented it in truth and love. I don't know of many ministries trying to reach witches but there are many out there that have written them off.

Our internet visitors ranged from former occultists, to church folk who needed us to share a word with them about different myths running rampant in the churches pertaining to witches and occultists. To sum it up, we're just trying to do God's will as we talked to the people who stopped in.

I must say that getting together with Christian ex-witches to teach and reach out to pagans on the web sometimes felt like we were painting targets on ourselves, but nothing quite compares to getting abused by the brethren for taking the gospel to the lost. At times, it felt like we were catching it from both ends.

I've met some really nice people who are truly following Jesus. They encourage my faith and help me to believe in the mission of His people. Yes, in case you haven't noticed, how you behave affects those around you, and their perception of Jesus.

## Addressing the Brethren

A word to those brethren who live in fear of witches and other occultists... God is bigger than they are. To the brethren that feel there is no such thing as magick, witches, or the occult it is time to go back and read God's Word. Please pay special attention to Exodus and Acts.

The next thing that I will address has happened to me more than once. Even if you doubt what God's Word says about witchcraft and occult practices, please refrain from tempting former occultists to sin by requesting them to perform magick for morbid curiosity. If you will not believe God's Word, why would you believe any sign provided through magick? And if you are truly following my Lord Jesus, why would you want someone to fall into sin?

Bottom line... the transition from a magickal path to following Jesus is hard enough without the church folk making it even more difficult. Besides, the job of the Church is to tell people about Jesus and help them live a life pleasing to Him, not to create witches by driving a wedge between Jesus and the lost. Yes, people have free will to choose Jesus or to walk away from Him... but why should we behave in such a way as to push people away or cause them to question our faith?

## A Time to Heal

More recently, I seem to have been sidelined and I believe that God is giving me time for learning and some emotional healing. I acknowledge now that most of my anger at the Church all this time has been displaced anger. The wounds are real, but it is not the fault of the Church as a whole nearly so much as it is my fault and the fault of those who are misleading my brethren. Then there is the fact that the Church is not the enemy. This has been a rough lesson for me, but a necessary one. I had to deal with the fallout and hurt from the actions of different churches across the country as they improperly dealt with former witches and occultists. I had to remember that they have been deceived and are not the root cause of the pain.

When Satan can keep the Church off balance and fearful, then he can use them to further his aims, and one of those is to keep people away from Jesus. One thing I learned from Scripture and God's people in the years I've been following Jesus, I am comforted in knowing that even in the valley that we are going through Jesus is walking with us and will deliver us out in His time. Meanwhile, I have learned much from the writings of the Christian Sisters Elliot, Ten Boom, the Brothers Moody, Torrey, and especially John Rice. The lessons I learned from them underscored what it means to follow Jesus and have His power working through your life.

The inclusion of Fundamentalist John Rice may surprise you, but his works are amazing as he wrote the most comprehensive work on the power of the Holy Spirit I have ever read. The current editor of Sword of the Lord publication has probably since forgotten, but I enjoyed the look on his face when I told him that if he would keep it in print, I would recommend it to every ex-witch I spoke to. The title is 'The Power of Pentecost' so I've kept my end of the bargain and as far as I know it is still available from Sword of the Lord.

## The Bottom Line

The bottom line is that God loves us and is still willing to work in our lives much like He did during biblical times. I do not know what God has in store for me going forward, but what I know is that I need to trust Him. Remembering that it is not who I am or was... but rather, who Jesus is; that is, what really matters as we walk through this life is to do our best to tell people about the gospel... not just in words, but in our lives.

# CHAPTER SIXTEEN

## April Dryburgh

April was introduced to the tarot at an early age setting the stage for her future occult involvement. After exploring Wicca, Buddhism and Shamanism, she became certified as a level one Reiki practitioner and took a job at a psychic hotline. New Age Spirituality had become her way of life until a hidden secret from her past would uncover the root of unforgiveness.

I lived in the small town of Fairplay, Colorado and attended a Christian daycare in a church when I was about four years old. That was until my mom got really mad one day when they frightened my brother and me by having someone dress up like Satan come in and we were told to pray to Jesus to make Satan leave, which of course we did and the costumed guy left. My dad was an atheist when he and Mom were first together but he took us to different churches occasionally as he explored different faiths.

My parents divorced when I was five years old, so I lived with my mom and saw my dad on weekends and holidays. Our household was dysfunctional as my mom struggled with depression, coupled with the challenging lifestyle of working graveyard shifts, so she slept during the day which resulted in a lack of parental supervision with no set boundaries. When I was nine years old, my mother's brother got divorced and came to stay with us which was the worst thing that could happen in my young life. In the middle of the night he came into my bedroom and molested me, but out of fear, I kept this terrible secret hidden deep inside until years later.

## Indoctrination

My mom was into the New Age and dabbled in occult practices. She was the first person to introduce me to tarot cards when I was still very young. She took me along with her to metaphysical bookstores where she bought books on witchcraft and sometimes she would share with me what she read. She often did tarot readings and even bought me my first tarot deck. I didn't really know much about it at that point and never really used them.

My mom suddenly returned to the Catholic Church when I was about eleven and took me and my siblings along with her. I am still unclear about what exactly made her return to church, but it had something to do with a sudden fear of the tarot cards and witchcraft, and it was obvious something had occurred causing her to recognize the demonic evil around them. She threw away all the tarot cards and enrolled us kids in Catholic religious education classes. Even though I was not the best-behaved student in class, I still wanted to be baptized and become part of the church. I enjoyed wearing a "Warrior for Christ" t-shirt; it had a good yet rebellious feel to it.

Even so, sin was still prevalent in my life and my behaviors of sometimes acting out sexually or using vulgar language obviously came from my traumatic childhood experience. At some point I smoked cigarettes and experimented with drugs. I also experimented with witchcraft and developed a fascination with divination, even trying to communicate with the dead through Ouija boards, as my sin spiritually blinded me.

When I was fifteen years old, I was devastated as my own brother sexually assaulted me and I confided what had happened to my school counselor who called Social Services and the police. My brother denied it and sadly, my mother believed him. Social Services placed me with my grandparents, who after about a week sent me to live with my dad, who over time let me go live with a high school friend. During all this turmoil, I stopped attending church services and got more into drinking as I was angry and not doing well emotionally... numbing my mind with alcohol and bringing my internal pain to the surface by cutting myself. Looking back, I think that the heavy metal music, in part, inspired me to start cutting, and I eventually ended up in a mental hospital, then a group home.

## Exploring Wicca

In the meantime, my older sister whom I looked up to was off at college and had met some Wiccans who introduced her to the Craft and Wiccan spirituality. She wanted to help me so she sent me letters and came for a visit telling me all about Wicca, lending me books and teaching me spells. She also gave me a lot of tips and advice concerning using magick for protection which was very appealing to me at the time as I desired it, as well as power and control in my current situation. I never realized the unsafe ground I was treading as I was moving further away from God in that way.

When I began dabbling, I convinced my sister that I was a psychic and even though my mom had returned to church; she didn't dissuade me... even thinking I had a gift for it. My tarot readings impressed my friends, and it wasn't long before I charged for them. I often went to the metaphysical bookstore and talked to people about Wicca, the tarot and learning about Norse "gods and goddesses," who were of particular interest to me.

Someone invited me to a Samhain celebration that was hosted annually at a Universalist church in Denver by a friend I met at a coffee shop. I went that year in a dress that a friend of a friend made and I sported a lot of metaphysical jewelry. They held a circle that I took part in. We were a large group of people standing in a circle holding hands, casting a protection spell and inviting "good" spirits to come and join us. We chanted and then it was shared that the afterlife and the physical world were connected and open to each other because of the special day it was.

By the time I was seventeen I had a job at a grocery store and my own apartment. I still did a lot of drinking and cutting but the more I got into the occult, the more I thought it was helping me. Finally, it appeared my life was going in the right direction.

That was until I was aghast to discover that someone stole some money from me and I couldn't make the full month's rent. I got really depressed, so I spent the rest of what I had on alcohol and drugs and, being I didn't want to end up on the street or back at my moms where my brother still lived, I got drunk and slit my wrist deeply in a suicide attempt. They took me to the emergency room and, thank God, I survived, but to this day I carry a very large ugly scar on my left arm because of it. I got a lot of help in the hospital and started my walk to sobriety.

## Psychic Hotline

I met a customer at the grocery store where I worked and we became friends. He worked at a psychic line and with his help, got me a job there. We worked out of an office instead of using home phone lines, so I got to know many people who were into various types of "spirituality" and occultism. I learned much from my co-workers about the many spiritual paths such as Buddhism and Shamanism. I studied the basics of astrology and practiced various meditations. I learned Reiki and was even certified as a level one practitioner. It wasn't just dabbling anymore. Working at the psychic line was now a major part of my life as I did nothing other than learn and perform various occult practices. The Universal Life Church of California, which basically bestows mail order credentials ordained me and several of my friends during my time working at the psychic line. I learned about the "law of attraction" before the book "The Secret" ever came out. A friend gave me a copy of "The Bloodline of the Holy Grail" which seemed logical in its heretical claims and false translations of Scripture. I worked there about three years before it closed down around 1998.

I met my daughter's dad around that time and we became legally married just before her birth in 2002. By then I had straightened out my life with the help of a friend I met working at the psychic line. I wasn't drinking anymore and wasn't anywhere near the emotional wreck I had been as my life now centered on my new family, and I was determined to have a good, moral, and safe environment for my daughter as I wanted better for her than what I experienced in my childhood. I still had my tarot cards but gradually drifted away from New Age spirituality. I no longer consider myself to be Christian, Wiccan, pagan, or anything really, although I guess that would have made me agnostic, but I rejected that label too. I was obsessed about religion; mostly relating to things from a pagan or secular viewpoint. Around 2008 I watched the "Zeitgeist" Christian conspiracy documentary which convinced me that Jesus didn't even exist and I called myself an atheist. Looking back, that's interesting since I didn't claim to be a Christian and even called on false gods. It's clear to me now that some part of me knew that Jesus is God, and there is no other name by which we are saved.

In January 2009 my grandma passed away. It was just before the funeral when my uncle asked my daughter if she knew who Jesus is and her reply was simply, "God". It stunned me! I had no clue how she came up with that answer since I had not raised her in the Christian faith. My uncle smiled and told her she was right. I quickly inquired, "Who told you Jesus is God?" She replied, "No one, I just knew that." By the end of our stay, she had memorized The Lord's Prayer.

## The Terrible Nightmare

Later that same year my dad wrote an article for The Examiner Website about the spiritual dangers of Ouija boards. He included in his article about my brother and I having used Ouija boards in our youth and the troubles that ensued. My dad wrote his suspicions that my brother could be demonically possessed and I thought he was just making excuses for the scary and evil person my brother was. I hated my brother and had harbored unforgiveness since I was fifteen years old and at the time of reading the article I was thirty-three. I had no idea how much hatred was separating me from the love of God.

That night I had a terrible nightmare. I was standing face to face with my brother and could see the demon in him looking back at me. I could see this horrible, evil, vile and frightening face that I didn't believe in, staring back at me. It was determined to kill me and take both my brother and I to hell. I called out for Jesus to help for the first time in fifteen years and I even prayed for my brother. Once awake, I continued to pray throughout the entire day. I told no one, but prayed, "Jesus, if this is real, if there is a demon or demons, please expose them and cast them out." It was only a day later that I received the e-mail from my sister with the news that my brother was arrested for firing tracer rounds from a rifle over a busy highway. Thank God he hurt no one, but I never would have thought this is how my prayers would be answered, yet I knew they had been.

I became consumed with the ongoing saga of my brother's story and spent time googling his name, reading his MySpace page, other articles, and people's comments. I came across an article where my mom was quoted, "He didn't do the things they say he did, but we don't know how to prove it." This caused me to flashback into all the anger I had towards my mom for her constant denial in my teen years. She didn't believe me when I had finally told her what my brother and uncle had done which caused a lasting rift between us for years and I had to learn how to forgive her. This time though the evidence against him was overwhelming, and they sentenced him to five years in prison.

I spiraled down further into depression and my husband was no support, hardly wanting to be around me, let alone talk to or support me. He emotionally withdrew from our already troubled marriage which depressed and angered me all the more. I was sinking into a dark state and I was not emotionally present for my daughter which was bothering me most of all. My aunt and uncle asked if I would go speak to a friend of theirs who was a priest. At first, I refused because he was a priest. I was looking for a "secular" counselor, but when I looked up the choices from the insurance company website something hit me with a desperate and overwhelming feeling that was crippling. I just knew... I had to go see this priest.

The priest was visiting from India and had only been in the United States a few years working on his counseling degree. I met with him on one condition... that he not mention religion or try to convert me. My time in counseling with him was short but life altering. I spent one hour with him in the church and after that hour, all my depression, insomnia and nightmares had vanished and over time, I felt the Holy Spirit was drawing me back to Jesus.

## His Love Broke Through

Experiencing His authentic light and love jarred my memory to an earlier time when I felt His Spirit reaching out to me. Ironically, it was at the funeral of a friend whose life had been tragically cut short. I hoped to project light into this room filled with anger and despair, when suddenly I felt something far greater than I could ever emit. God's love so filled the place that my own efforts seemed lame in comparison. I would explain the difference of my light compared to God's... as the difference between a single match versus the light of the sun.

At that time, I still had doubts and questions because everything I thought I knew and learned contradicted what I was experiencing now, but the draw was so strong that it overpowered my doubts, and I attended church and read the Bible. I think I started to realize God was stirring my heart while listening to the Wednesday evening talks at church, and after calling a friend who had worked with me at the psychic hotline who had converted to Christianity a few years earlier. She recommended a one year Bible which she had read and was very supportive in my transition back to Christ.

I personally prayed for Jesus to be with me, live in my heart, and forgive my sins and to help me grow closer to Him. I frequently pray to Jesus and for the Holy Spirit's guidance thanking Him for His presence. At first I thought it had something to do with the priest I first met with, but while I'm thankful for him, I know he was only used as an instrument of the Holy Spirit as I finally understand who Jesus is and what He did for me.

One of my parish priests encouraged me to throw away my tarot cards, all my books and pagan possessions. He suggested that I burn them but I didn't, I just threw them in the trash. There was a dream catcher that I didn't want to throw away and my priest offered to buy me something else, even better to replace it so I threw it away and he bought me a stained glass image of Jesus, known as "the Divine Mercy." It is beautiful and, being so appropriate, I never regretted throwing away the dream catcher.

## The Challenge

For those who are actively involved in the occult, I challenge you to examine honestly why you have rejected Jesus. If you don't believe Jesus is real, I implore you to look into it further. You can find the truth and Jesus is true, He is God. If you don't believe the Bible says that, then you have not read it. I pray that your heart will be softened. God does not withhold good things from His children. When He has commanded against something, it is because it is not good for us. The lie that Satan has told us is that we can, of our own power, have more, and that God is keeping something from us. That is what he told Adam and Eve, that is what he still tells people today and we buy it. The truth is God created us out of love and He wants us to have every good thing. When we sin we separate ourselves from God and we must repent and turn back to Him. We live in a fallen world in which evil and sin abound because of sin, but there is a way back to God and back to the perfection of his creation in Heaven, the only way back is through Jesus Christ, His Son.

# CHAPTER SEVENTEEN

## Carrie Christian

*Carrie was just an innocent child when Satan captivated her mind by planting a seed of doubt that would be become the catalyst to her descent into darkness. Over time, her spiritual quest led her to the path of an Eclectic Witch where for twenty-years she blended Celtic witchcraft, Luciferianism, Satanism, and Voodoo into her form of witchcraft. Carrie was appointed high priestess over a witchcraft coven, while unbeknownst to its members, secretly worked with a satanic coven until three simple words paved the way for breaktkthrough.*

It all began with an event used by Satan to lure me into occult activities which led to my descent into darkness. In the initial years of my life, my family lived over eight hundred miles away from my grandparents. Although the distance was lengthy, my parents would bring me and my siblings to visit them yearly. My papaw, an avid smoker, worked in the coal mines all his life and became ill with lung cancer. All my last memories of my papaw were of oxygen tubes, difficulty breathing, and frailty... not very pleasant ones of someone you loved.

At seven, my papaw passed away and my family returned home to attend his funeral. My parents did not allow my younger sister or I to go as I assume they did not want us traumatized to see him like that. I was to have spent the night of the funeral with my grandmother at her home. My grandmother retired into her bedroom and closed the door. I entered the spare bedroom and fixed an extra blanket on my bed when I heard the floorboards of the old house creak as if someone were walking in the dining room. Seeking reassurance, I called out, "I'm going to bed granny, I got cold and got another blanket." She did not respond. I repeated myself as I did not want to upset her for still being up. Again, no response. Curious, I walked to the doorway... and froze, as I saw my papaw coming out of the dining room and walking down the hall. He stood tall with no oxygen tubes, healthy, dressed in his usual flannel shirt and carrying his favorite coffee cup. I had goosebumps as he continued down the hall and into the bathroom diagonal to my room. He placed his coffee cup down, put both hands on the sides of the sink and stared into the mirror. Not wanting him to catch me staring, I turned around with my back to the hall, but when I looked back, he had vanished. I walked into the bathroom calling, "Papaw, Papaw". but I only saw his coffee cup sitting on the sink with steam rising out. I ran into my grandmother's room and told her I had seen papaw in the bathroom. She did not believe in such and scolded me. With that, I had her call my parents to come get me. My parents arrived, and I left crying. They gave me the silent treatment when I told them what I had witnessed. Even as an adult, I never stayed at that house again and when I would visit her, I would wander down that hall and felt the eeriness of something watching me.

## Satan's Bait

As for my childhood, my parents raised me up in church. We moved back to my grandparents' hometown and attended the local Pentecostal church down the street from our home. I sang in the choir and attended youth group throughout my teen years. Every Sunday I attended Sunday school. My mother and I would assist with church dinners, cleaning the church and help coordinate various church functions. Church goers and Christian influence surrounded me. When I was twelve, a foreboding remembrance of seeing my papaw after his death resurfaced. Visions of him walking down the hall haunted my dreams and caused me to question my faith. I told my Sunday school teacher about my dreams, hoping she would give me an answer, but she told me I hadn't seen my papaw, but a demon and not to wonder about it again. She warned of the dangers of seeking answers about ghosts and demons. She gave no further explanation or teaching, just a calloused rebuke "do NOT dwell on this and that's that." The answer hit me hard. why would a demon appear as my papaw... this made no sense? In my mind, I had seen my "Papaw", not some snarling dark demon figure. I was never told that Satan appeared as an angel of light, presenting himself as innocent and familiar to draw me away from God. Had someone explained it, even at that young age, it could have helped me understand. (In order that Satan doesn't take advantage of us; for we are NOT ignorant of his schemes - 2 Corinthians 2:11 NASB) Satan used this confusion within me to set up a stumbling block that would lead me off the Christian path.

Unable to find answers, I strayed away from my faith... and fell right into the trap Satan had set for me. The Bible warns us to "be sober, be vigilant: because your adversary the devil, as a roaring lion, walketh about, seeking whom he may devour." (1 Peter 5:8 (KJV)) Satan sought to create doubt and isolation, leading me away from the Christians in my life, leaving me vulnerable to his attacks. Sadly, I nor those around me, recognized the danger signs. I still attended church with my mother, but inside, Satan tormented me.

## The Devil's Advocate

That summer while I was hanging out at the elementary school where local teens hung out to use the basketball hoops and concrete steps for skateboarding, a group of kids befriended me. One guy, who I will call "Jeremy", became my friend. He would skateboard with me at the school and we would hang out on my porch in the evenings. As we grew closer, I confessed to Jeremy about what happened in my childhood and that I wondered why my papaw came as he did. One evening, he brought several books to my house. and sat out on the porch steps as he shared them with me. The books included The Necronomicon (a book that tells how to summon demonic entities), which he told me I could borrow and that these books would help me find the answer to the questions I sought.

The books scared me and I refused to take them. Jeremy then told me about Ouija boards and how they would help. I told him that my parents would not allow me to have one. Jeremy informed me how to make one myself and showed me a drawing of one he made. He told me a handmade one would do the same as having an actual wooden board and also showed me how to make a planchette out of a piece of cardboard, in which I did and kept under my mattress. Jeremy made himself available for my questions, even calling me on the phone several times a week. I was unaware at the time that Jeremy practiced Satanism. When I asked him why he had such books and how he knew all he did, he told me it was his belief. At first, it frightened me and I avoided him for weeks. My Christian upbringing was screaming at me to stay away, however, I ended up falling into temptation. I just wanted peace of mind and didn't care where the answers came from. Later on, Jeremy confessed to me what he practiced, and that he was in it with his friends. They told me about writing out "contracts" to Satan, by cutting themselves and signing them in blood before putting them in the river. I could hardly believe they would do such a thing. Later, Jeremy would become the high priest of the coven he is part of.

## Paranormal Activity

During my teen years I fell deeper into the occult by using the Ouija board I had made, tarot cards I purchased at our local mall, performing spells and reading books on witchcraft. On my bedroom floor, I drew a pentagram then covered it with my carpet to keep it hidden from my parents. My parents never knew all the occult items hidden in varies places of my room. Yet through it all, I still attended church with my mom until my parents had trouble in their marriage and my mother quit church. I was living two separate lives. From the outside, people saw me as the good little straight-A church girl that never got into trouble or misbehaved. The one who lived in the nice house on the nice street and had such a good home life. On the inside, I fell deeper into darkness, and no one took notice.

This was a pivotal point in my occult path when what I was

practicing became more than real as I saw demonic physical manifestations. The first, I saw a little girl standing behind me in the bathroom mirror. I turned around to look; she was standing against the wall in the upstairs landing. She stood about four foot tall, had stringy blonde ashy hair and wore a long dirty white Victorian nightgown with an untied dirty white bonnet. Her eyes were dark, her skin was a whitish-gray and her face looked sunk in at her cheekbones, as if she was malnourished. The little girl stared at me but never spoke, as I stood there frozen. In what seemed like minutes, she turned to her right and walked into the next room. I followed, but she disappeared.

The second manifestation happened when I was laying in my bed with the light on. I lived in a historic home with twelve foot vaulted ceilings. This dark figure entered my room and stood at the end of my bed. This ominous presence's shoulders touched the ceiling, making its head bend over. I laid there paralyzed... unable to move, speak, or cry out for my parents. It leaned down and hovered its face over mine. I closed my eyes. tears ran down the side of my cheek. Its breath smelled of rancid flesh and its condensation was upon my face. My heart pounded in my chest and the encounter felt like it lasted an eternity. Once this subsided and I could move, I screamed as loud as I could for my mom and dad. I told them what had happened and my mom called Sister Holley who lived across the street from us. Brother Holley was a pastor and an evangelist. They had me come over the next morning and tell them what had occurred. They came with me back to my house and anointed my room and hung prayer clothes over the door, windows, closet, and even put one in my pillow. After that, I saw nothing else inside my room, but I would hear something growl from outside of my door and could sense the darkness there. This harassment continued until I moved out.

## Out of the Broom Closet

The day after I turned eighteen, I got married and was expecting my first child. Now that I was out from under my parents' roof, I became an openly practicing witch. My marriage was not a good one. My husband had grown up in the Catholic church as a child, but after the death of his father at a young age he no longer believed in God. He was an alcoholic and physically, emotionally and mentally abusive. During our marriage he kicked me in the face with steel-toed boots and had my ribs broken. I ended up leaving to save my life. At the age of twenty-five, I became a single mother on my own with two children. The hurt I experienced caused me to fall into depression and I drank to help cope.

I now had my own home and could set things up the way I wanted. I had an altar set up inside my home which I proudly displayed in the parlor. The lighted curio cabinet in the hall held all my deity statues when they weren't being used in ritual. I incorporated various forms of religions into my witchcraft, including Luciferianism, Satanism, Voodoo and Celtic Witchcraft. I even had a granite statue of Lucifer. My occult practices grew deeper as I studied occult writings, did divination for others, and performed various forms of necromancy. By now I had had several ritual robes I kept in my closet and many books on witchcraft which I kept on a large bookshelf. I marked my body with eleven occult tattoos, including the one representing the unholy trinity on my wrist. On weekends while my kids were visiting with their dad, I would go hiking. I'd bring my grimoires with me and sit on a rock in the stream while working on spells. If it was an occult practice such as Chakra healings to pendulum readings... you name it, I would try it.

A fellow witch introduced me to Derick. He had been a high priest for over thirty years and the knowledge he conveyed upon meeting him intrigued me and we promptly became friends. With his guidance, we started a coven with several other solitary witches I knew in the area. Derick designated me high priestess because of my years of experience. I trained the others on how to set up altars, supplied what they needed to perform rituals and provided a list of materials they needed to make or purchase. I served as their high priestess for thirteen years and initiated others into the Craft. Once we established the coven, Derek returned to his own coven and became our elder who occasionally came to our gatherings and provided guidance when needed.

## The Satanic Coven

During this time, I not only practiced witchcraft but unbeknownst to Derick, I had reconnected with Jeremy and was taking part in rituals and festivities with his satanic coven. I would invoke spirits that gave me certain abilities and perform rituals asking them to use me, which they did. I had no shame. Whatever I had to do to get someone into the satanic coven, I would do. If it required sex, I would invoke the spirits of lust to lure them in. If it required becoming their dear friend, I'd befriend them. Whatever Satan required, I did. I cut myself to acquire blood, and I willingly bore those marks. I studied in my free time. Anything dark and forbidden, I wanted. Once I performed an invocation, asking the spirit that represented lust and desire to use me, therefore I did the required ritual, gave my blood, and took the ritual bath. I soon felt the cold consuming presence go into me. It's something I will never forget... giving up the rights to my body for this demonic entity. This demon used my body for debauchery too many times to remember.

Also during my years in the satanic coven, I took part in sex rituals. If it were against God, we did it and their were no limits. Once I was so violently raped it took my body weeks to recover. Sex meant nothing. It was just a "do what thou wilt" thing, be it rituals, parties, or at their beck and call. One of these sexual encounters resulted in my pregnancy, which ended in abortion. Now that I am saved, it is the most hurtful and heart wrenching part of my past. It's the one choice I regret the most. Satan used these memories for years to make me shameful and hold hatred towards myself, even to the point of becoming suicidal. It still brings tears to my eyes as I write this.

It got to where I was such a heavy drinker I would have to take a shot of liquor to sleep at night. One time I recall sitting on my floor in front of my dresser and had written a poem about my suicide and what my death would be like. On my leg I had a razor to slice my wrists open. What kept me from it? I will say it was God. The second most vivid attempt was putting a loaded pearl-handled pistol that was my grandfather's in my mouth and trying so hard to pull back that trigger. I couldn't do it, all I say again, it had to be God.

Even after all this, I dug deeper into witchcraft and Satanism to the point of scaring myself. I could hear these demons speak and sense them around me. I had no fear in what I was doing. Whatever they called for, I willingly obeyed even to the point of death.

But God...

I love those two words, and for good reason!

### The Battle for My Soul

Satan had a plan of destruction set for me. He had me deep in his clutches and I was his willing servant. But God had another plan, one set before my mother conceived me, that was not for evil but for good, to give me a future and hope. Little did I realize that God was fighting for my soul. There are so many times I came close to death, so many times violence should have taken my life. I should NOT be here sharing this testimony, but God wanted to give me life. That is an overwhelming, beautiful thing that just floods my heart with gratitude to God. He never gave up. When no one came to witness or to show me Jesus, when everyone ran the opposite direction, God was still there. He saw through my darkness and knew the beautiful prodigal child He loved. The Holy Spirit convicted me about six months before I got saved and I lost all desire for darkness during this time. God was working a miracle in my life.

The final ritual I performed remains ingrained in my memory. I set my altar up with my deity statues, candles, pentagram, incense, water and salt. The pentagram rug lay on the floor in front of the altar. After my ritual cleansing bath, I put on my black robe with a green Celtic pentacle on the back and came into the circle, called the "guardians", and performed the ritual. Kneeling in the pentagram, I was chanting when I heard these words "Who are you even praying to?" I opened my eyes and looked around. No one was there, but I kept hearing those words over and over to the point of disgust and I got up, blew out the candles, picked up my rug, put the robe in the closet and went to sit on my porch. My stomach felt queasy, like I wanted to vomit. Most of that night I sat on my porch in the darkness, shaking my head in shame.

The next few months, I grew a distaste for witchcraft and had an overwhelming feeling of heaviness. An enormous snake chased me in my dreams, trying to swallow me alive. On another occasion, I saw a dark elderly woman-like figure sitting in a Victorian Queen Anne chair I had in my bedroom; I knew she was the crone goddess and always thought she was friendly, only this time I felt as if she wanted to claw my eyes out. Not being able to sleep, I tossed and turned night after night, not even wanting to set up my altar or work a spell. Nothing seemed to give me any pleasure anymore. I felt numb and uneasy with my belief and lifestyle. This is the best way I can put into words. Even the alcohol seemed to make me ill instead of numbing my pain or aiding my sleep.

### Jesus Loves You

While working at a place that helped abused women. I met Pastor Cook. Most of the time, I got into confrontations with clergy and Christians and I admittedly started it. Most of them looked down on me, judged and despised me, calling me an abomination. This pastor would not argue which only frustrated me. He asked if I attended church anywhere, and I would just ignore him. He was always smiling and I could not stand him. The spirits inside me did not like being around him. I would try to start arguments, and his only reply would be "Jesus loves you". That drove me crazy! I would give my crass reply "No He does not", but he would continue to say "Jesus loves you" He later told me he felt led to just repeat those words and repeat them he did.

I asked, after spewing out my anger about God, why he didn't get mad... why he didn't argue... here I am, I'm sitting here talking down about your God and you don't defend him, what is wrong with you? He would reply, "I can't get mad at you. Jesus loves you so much." I wanted to scream. At night, his words, "Jesus loves you" would echo through my mind. Over the next few months Pastor Cook continued to share his faith, and I told him I was a witch and a high priestess. He talked about Jesus and His love and never once expressed anger. One night I reluctantly went to a church service, more out of spite than anything else, I thought it would all prove to be a lie.

## Take Me to the King

Even after walking into that church service with resentment and spite in my heart, the song that was being sung that night pierced my heart. "Take me to the King" by Tamara Mann. It prompted questions that swirled within my mind... asking God, "How can you love me?, I bowed to Satan, hated and cursed your name, how can you still love me?" I didn't feel God's anger or rejection... what I felt was love. A warmth overtook me. A light that pierced right through me. Tears fell from my eyes as I walked up to the altar that night and gave my heart back to God, repenting and renouncing witchcraft. Ironically, I entered the church service as a witch with anger in my heart, but God met me in that pew. He was waiting to wrap his arms around me to bring me home. At last, I was being set free.

## Spiritual House Cleaning

The pastor explained the need for me to get rid of all occult items so a lady minister from the church visited my home to help me bag it all up. We searched through every room from top to bottom. She brought the bags out of the house and took them to a private home where they were burnt. They sent me photos of the fire, and you can see faces in the flames and the ministers who were present said there was a strange, horrific indescribable smell. I knew what they meant, knowing what all those bags contained. I went through deliverance. It is difficult to put into words, but I experienced a physical sickness, I felt dread and unrest like a knot inside my chest that just would not go away. I knew this was an internal demonic manifestation. The pastor who performed my deliverance and two other ministers who were present told me I cursed, scratched, repeatedly plunged myself on the floor and even tried to grab one minister by the throat. All I can remember was starting the day in prayer and ending it vomiting. I was so tired but knew something was different. That night was the first night in many years I could lie down and sleep and felt at peace. After I gave my life back to God, I poured all the alcohol I had in my house down the drain. I had to pray through the urges at first, but God took it away after my deliverance and healed me from that addiction. I no longer had a desire to drink and my need for alcohol left. I no longer had suicidal thoughts and the demonic spirits that wanted to take my life, and further the satanic agenda I had served for so long, were no more!

After all this, there was still a lingering ominious presence in my home because of the rituals performed there. My eleven-year-old daughter, was sitting in the living room watching a movie, when the French doors closed on their own. No matter how many lights were on... a darkness remained and I could sense something watching me. A group of ministers came and prayed over my home and I had no more issues since. God has His angels encamped around me and my children; He has filled my house with peace and joy.

I had to let God do His work in me. You cannot serve two masters. I love God's Word and I spend a lot of time in it. Satan tries to fight me, but he is a defeated foe. I keep a constant guard on my mind and my heart, filling it with the things of God. Jesus says "seek and you SHALL find" (Matthew 7:7 (KJV)) and when you seek Him, He promises you SHALL find Him. God has changed my thoughts and attitude. He delivered me from witchcraft, Satanism and alcoholism. He forgave me for sins so dark I cannot even put them in this testimony; my sins were nailed to the cross and covered in Jesus' blood. Even my physical countenance has changed. He has placed a great calling on my life and I will proclaim victory over the enemy in every church He sends me to and to every person He puts in my path. I am so thankful to God that since my salvation, my girls have been attending church with me.

## A Message of Hope

There is nothing too hard for God and no one that He cannot reach. I pray that someone finds hope in my words. I understand these words are hard to swallow and my story is what nightmares are made of... but I also know Jesus saves! There is freedom in Him and POWER IN HIS BLOOD! I am a living testimony of mercy He left the ninety-nine to find... a broken, disgraced witch to save and bring home to Him again! All glory be unto God!

Through Christ I have the victory, and it is only through Him I can proclaim, "It is well with my soul".

"... so that you may proclaim the excellency of Him who has called you out of darkness into His marvelous light: for you once were not a people, but now you are the people of God; you had not received mercy, but now you have received mercy." 1 Peter 2:9,10 (NASB)

## CHAPTER EIGHTEEN

—∞—

## Shari (Hadley) Pruitt

S*hari dabbled with occult games as a child but it was her faltering faith while attending college that led her to embrace goddess spirituality. After her dedication into Wicca, she spent the next nine years following the solitary Wiccan path, until tragedy struck and an unexpected visitor showed up at her door.*

I could hear my mother's rage building from my bedroom where I huddled in my bed, crying. As an eight-year-old who had witnessed countless scenes like the one developing, I knew she would lash out at my older brother, Kendall.

Various forms of abuse were served to us daily as I was growing up. By the time I was five, I believed this kind of life was normal. I had no way of knowing there was anything else. My father thought he was too educated to be duped into believing the mythology of any religion and my mother was preoccupied with her mental illness.

Now, as I waited for her to assault Kendall with her growing rage, I desperately wanted someone to whom I could run to for help, protection, and love. But where could I turn? The only Christian influence in my life was my paternal grandmother. She took my brother and me to a small country church infrequently for about three years. After she developed Alzheimer's, we stopped going to church completely.

But crying in my bed that horrible night, I recalled the pictures of Jesus in my children's Bible. He was surrounded by children—happy children who ran into His safe, outstretched arms. I wanted to be a part of that picture more than anything. I sat on the bed in my darkened room and prayed. As tears streamed down my face, I prayed for Jesus' love and protection, begging to have someone, anyone, to care for me.

I slept more peacefully that night than I ever had before, and I awoke early the next morning to the rising sun. It filled me with a quiet calm I had never known. I knew there had been a change in me, but I could not figure out what that change was.

### A Reason to Live

After, a few years I forgot about this event in my life. In fact, I would not realize the power of that prayer or experience that peace again until twenty-two years later.

The situation in my home did not change after that night when I had asked Jesus to love me. Time passed, the abuse and neglect continued, and I eventually became suicidal. I was full of shame and an indescribable self-loathing. I saw death as an escape—the only escape. I fantasized about the various ways to achieve the means to my end, but in my childlike manner, I always found an excuse not to go through with it.

In the end there were only two things that kept me alive. One was the fear I would burn in hell for committing suicide. I didn't think Jesus would want me to commit such an act. The second was the cat. I rationalized, "Who will feed Twinklepaws if you kill yourself, Shari?" I loved that cat—she kept me alive for years.

Growing up in rural Missouri with not even a gas station within ten miles of our home... the woods, the Osage River and my own imagination provided me with most of the entertainment in my life. I was curious about spiritual matters, and garnered most of my information from my mother and aunt's New Age books, fantasy novels, experimenting with the Ouija board, and old school role-playing games, such as Dungeons and Dragons. This was life before home computers, cell phones and internet, and with no other guidance, I found myself slowly drawn to the occult.

## Craft Curriculum

My journey into paganism began when I was a student at the local state university. My flimsy Christian faith was wishy-washy at best, so to have it challenged by intellectuals who did not believe in Christ caused those ungrounded beliefs to slide quickly into oblivion. I had always associated my identity as a Baptist. My husband and I had even married in the local Baptist church. Growing up where I did, I had no exposure to anyone but white Protestant Christians or apathetic non-believers. Now at the state university, I was suddenly thrown together with people from different races, ethnicities, countries, and religious beliefs. My feeble identity crumbled under my own skepticism, and I soon found myself on a journey of discovery.

I soon realized people who questioned everything surrounded me, but in this environment of debate, they were also judgmental of those who did not agree with their viewpoints. I recall frequently Christians being unable to back up their beliefs due to lack of knowledge of apologetics. The non-Christian always seemed to "one up" the Christian, causing them to falter or stop the dialogue. Or worse yet, the Christian would confidently parrot something he or she had learned at church, something a Christian would understand and take for truth, but which non-Christians could quickly pick apart with philosophical questions, or merely respond to with a scoff.

Witnessing this time and again caused me to disassociate quickly with anything Christian. I viewed Christians as weak intellectually and spiritually. I easily developed an existential view of life. Merriam-Webster's Collegiate Dictionary defines existentialism as "a chiefly 20th century philosophical movement embracing diverse doctrines but centering on analysis of individual existence in an unfathomable universe and the plight of the individual who must assume ultimate responsibility for his acts of free will with no certain knowledge of what is right or wrong or good or bad."

Within two years of study at the university, I had chosen religious studies as my major. I wanted to dedicate my life to archaeology, its artifacts, and Carbon-14 dating. I loved researching history and enjoyed the thought of traveling the world and becoming wistfully lost in huge museums. Ironically, my focus of study was biblical archaeology; I enjoyed the Palestinian, Mediterranean, and Egyptian geographical areas over any other. So I became a student of the Bible—not as a believer, mind you, but as a cynical academic. In my mind, the Bible was a textbook full of interesting nuggets of history and geographical information. It was factually true from a humanistic standpoint, but the idea that it was the actual word of a God was utter nonsense to me.

I also took an American Indian religion course that spoke of animism—the belief that God is in every form of nature such as animals, rocks, trees, and rivers. I also realized just how cruel and intolerant Christians could be. We watched a video of a man from the Iroquois nation who discussed how Christians had murdered his ancestors in Canada. He described in detail how the mob of Christians kidnapped his kin, cheered during his family's crucifixion, and then took part in a communion where they drank the blood and ate the flesh of the poor dying natives, while quoting the Bible the entire time. It was a terrible testimony to hear, and I became physically nauseous watching it. This occurrence and many others fueled the fire of my smoldering repugnance toward Christianity.

## Rooted in Feminism

But what cinched my absolute abhorrence toward the Christian faith was my Women and Religion class. We studied the Bible from a woman's point of view with a very feminist professor. I idolized her and soon requested that she become my advisor just so I could see and talk with her more.

She assigned us several books for the class, but one book in particular will forever stand out in my mind: Text of Terror: Literary-Feminist Readings of Biblical Narratives by Phyllis Trible. In this book, Trible discusses four stories that depict the cruel treatment of women in the Bible; one example being Tamar's horrific rape.

So, by this point it was firmly set in my mind that Christians were ignorant, intolerant, murdering, rapist cannibals who worshiped a distant, unattainable male God that probably didn't even exist. Also, because my father had abused me, the idea of worshiping a God who was a father figure was nearly more than I could handle.

Three Wiccans were invited to speak during my Religious Studies class about their way of life. They explained how Wicca is a nature-based religion, involving a god and goddess; a balance of power between a male and female deity, no eternal punishment in hell, but simply a way to honor and draw energy from Mother Earth. I soon sought out more Wiccans and studied with incredible abandon. And so my nine year journey into the Craft began.

I was dedicated into my newfound spirituality and soon after entered into a trance-like state where I had a vision of walking towards a large gray stone altar in a open glen surrounded by a huge hedge of greenery. I then saw myself on the altar as a sacrifice to the gods. And then, the vision was gone. I was both terrified and perplexed but knew that was a sign that confirmed I was truly a Wiccan.

When it came to witchcraft, I did it all. I cast spells; I read tarot cards; I carved runes; I cast the sacred circle; I summoned spirits; I worshiped the sun, moon and stars; and I celebrated the pagan holidays and more. I did it all except join a coven. I was what you might call a solitary practitioner of The Craft, a lone witch. Each night I visualized a beautiful blue and sparkling silver mantel wrapping Randy, my son, and me in a blanket of healing, protection, and love. Visualization was my best mental tool as a Wiccan. There are tools of the trade: occult bookstores and catalogs are filled with them. I owned many magical items, but "advanced" witches know these are simply physical objects that help you focus your energies. Once you become practiced enough, you can create your focal points mentally. Then you project your built-up energies outward to effect change on your environment.

~ 225

## Door to My Heart

It was January 28, 2003, and my beloved husband Randy was late getting home. I knew it would take him time to run his errands that evening, but he was away too long. I was slowly becoming annoyed that he was not considerate enough to call. When one hour became over four hours and he was still not home, I knew there had to be a very good reason for him not to call. I imagined many terrible scenarios. I paced back and forth between his dinner that had long since grown cold and the kitchen window, which gave a perfect view of our driveway. I reassured myself that I regularly cast protection spells on my family, so everything had to be OK. There must be a good explanation for Randy's delay.

I felt my heart sink as I watched the state patrol cruiser stop at the end of my cul-de-sac. It shined a spotlight on all the mailboxes. I willed it to keep moving, to turn around. Instead, it pulled down my driveway with two men inside. I went out to meet them. The first man to step out of the cruiser was a familiar state trooper whose little girl was in my son's kindergarten class. For a split second I thought the man riding with him was Randy, but I was wrong.

The trooper stepped out of the patrol car first and asked with a pained expression if I was Shari Setzer, wife of Randy Setzer. I hesitantly replied yes. The second man opened his passenger's side door and slowly stepped out. He introduced himself as a chaplain for the Missouri State Highway Patrol. When a chaplain is brought to your door, it is never to bring good news. I fought to keep myself from slowly slipping into shock.

"I'm sorry to have to inform you," the trooper said in a matter-of-fact tone, "but Randy was in a car accident this evening. He did not survive." He had a sorrowful look.

"No. . ." I said in horror as my hands flew to my mouth.

"Yes," he said, fixing his eyes firmly to mine.

They had confirmed my worst fears—Randy had been killed in a car accident; he was never coming home again. The chaplain started up the steps to my home.

"No," I said, attempting to stop him. "We can't do this. My son is inside."

The chaplain stopped mid-step and asked, "You have a child?"

"Yes, it's his sixth birthday this weekend," I said. "We can't do this to him."

I was sobbing and irrational. I somehow thought if we stayed outside I would not have to face my child. And if I did not tell my child, then none of this would be real. I felt as cold and hollow as the January night air as we stepped inside.

A hundred thoughts filled my mind, not the least of which was, there is a Christian standing in my living room. It is going to look close enough and find me out. And that's what he was to me, an "It."

One of "them," the enemy, was there. Why? I thought. Where is she? Where is the goddess I have served so faithfully for nine years? I don't feel her, I don't see her, I have nowhere to turn. At this time in my life when I need her most. . . and she's not here?

Anger and doubt entered my mind. Does she exist? As my doubts rose, the door to Christianity slowly opened.

On any normal day I would have felt nothing but animosity toward the chaplain. I didn't see him as human, but as a threat, a thing, an intrusion, an "It." It was, after all, the worst of Its kind—a Christian, a man, and an authority equivalent to a high priest in my faith. It had power. It would judge, criticize and hate me.

I would have done anything to get rid of It. But this was no normal day. This was the day I had lost the one human being who had ever loved me completely. This was the day my husband, my best friend, my everything had died. I had bigger problems than a Christian standing in my living room; I had to tell my son his daddy was dead.

As I approached my five-year-old son, he sat on the couch looking intently at the police officer and the strange man standing in his home. He knew something was wrong. I sat next to him, filled with dread.

I looked up at It and spoke. "I don't know what to say. How do I tell him?" I asked sorrowfully.

At that moment It said an amazing thing. "I can do it for you," he offered.

He was willing to do this horrible duty for me. I now began to understand. He was there to help, to offer compassion not judgment, to show concern not hate. The Christian was no longer an It; he was human.

My hardened heart softened and the door to Christianity opened a little more. I replied, "No, I'll do it—it's my job." And I did. I told my little boy that his daddy was in a terrible car accident and that he was now in heaven with our dog who had died two years before. Many Wicca's believe in an afterlife, generally called Summerland, but for the sake of Christian in-laws and the Christian standing in front of me, I called it heaven.

My son showed little emotion at the news. He didn't comprehend the permanence or gravity of the situation. I had been prepared to comfort him, but instead I was the one comforted by the person I least expected: the Christian. He looked at me with genuine warmth and said three words, "You did good." Those three little words offered me more hope than he would ever know.

Telling my child he was fatherless was my first act as a single parent, and I finally realized the Christian was not there to chastise me, but to offer me support. The door to Christianity opened a little more.

I trembled as I flipped through my Rolodex, picking out people I needed to call. A dozen thoughts ran through my head: He just increased his life insurance yesterday... this can't be happening ... What am I going to tell his mother and sisters?... What am I going to do?

The Christian asked, "Is there someone you can call to come stay with you?"

We had no family in the area, so I settled on calling two of Randy's close friends from work.

As we waited for them to arrive, I nervously approached the patrolman with a difficult question. "Did Randy ... go... quickly?" I had horrible images of him lying on the pavement, suffering in terrible pain, calling my name.

"Yes," he said assuredly. "I want you to remember three things. He went quickly, he had on his seatbelt, and this wasn't his fault." He verbally stressed each point as he spoke.

This was a relief for me. It's sad to have to be thankful that your loved one died quickly, but he had always said he did not want to live in a vegetative state. And I never wanted him to suffer. Randy was also adamant about wearing seatbelts. He knew too many people who didn't wear them, and it always had bothered him. He was also a very safe driver and I could not remember the last time he had received a traffic violation. In fact, all the guys at his work constantly teased him about driving like "a little old lady." Some even stopped carpooling with him because he drove so slowly.

The evening news would soon be on, showing the accident, and I didn't want the family and friends to learn of Randy's death in that gruesome manner. So I made one horrible phone call after another, informing people of Randy's death. I was grateful for how the patrolman and the chaplain kept my son busy since I was in poor condition to tend to his needs. But I was worried about him, so I tried to check on him every few minutes, even though my mind was being pulled in a hundred different directions.

I remember one conversation vividly from that day with a loved one in Idaho. Cohen had been best man at our wedding and Randy loved him like a brother. Unbeknownst to me, Cohen had recently become born again.

I spoke to him through sobs, "Cohen," I said, "Randy has been killed in a car accident; I don't know what I'm going to do."

The first words he spoke were words no one had ever said in my thirty years on this earth. He said, "Shari, God loves you."

For just a few moments, time froze. The door to Christianity opened a little more. Randy's friends soon arrived at my home, and the patrolman and the Christian had to leave. But before he left, the Christian gave me his card in case I needed to find him. I still have that card.

## Unanswered Questions

I was too full of grief to sleep that night. I walked into my bedroom and took one look at the pagan altar on my dressing table, and I wanted to vomit. I was filled with loathing and revulsion. I opened the top drawer to my dresser, raked in all the idols, libation dishes, incense, and candles, and I then slammed the drawer shut. I was angry. Angry my protection spells did not work, angry that I did not sense my goddess, and angry that I felt I had nowhere to turn for comfort. I was wondering if I had simply been duped these past nine years. The door to Christianity opened a little more.

Question upon question filled my mind. What would I do with the body? Should I cremate him as he wished or should I succumb to pressure from family and have him embalmed as they wished? Who would do the memorial service? I knew no pastors.

My God, I am now a single mother. My God? What God? I was beginning to doubt such a being existed.

My provider was gone, How will I feed and clothe my child? My son's sixth birthday is in four days. What in the world am I going to do? How did Randy die? What were his injuries? Did he really not suffer as the patrolman said? How did the accident occur? Why is this happening to me... haven't I suffered enough in life?

All too soon the sun was rising on my widowhood and I had to make decisions on my own. I had met Randy when I was eighteen years old. From our first date I never saw anyone else. We were a team; that team was no more. My sister-in-law, brother-in-law, and father drove me to the local funeral home that was holding Randy's body. I sat in the front seat of their minivan wondering if it was all just a bad dream. Nothing felt tangible. I felt drained and hollow.

## The Powerless Reality

The fog of grief surrounded and tormented me. I felt so lost and forsaken—I didn't know where to seek comfort. There was nothing left for me in witchcraft, no spell or incantation to heal my pain. There was no book of knowledge from which I could derive wisdom.

I thought I created my own reality. If that were the case, then recreate this reality, Shari, I thought bitterly. Bring Randy back if you're so powerful. And while you're at it, since you're such a powerful being, Shari, create something. Let's start with a small pebble in your hand. I held my palm open and looked at it. Is a pebble too big? Then how about a single grain of sand? Still too hard? Then a speck of dust. Can't even create a single speck of dust, Shari? Then what makes you think you are so powerful that you can create your own reality.

The critique of my Neo-pagan belief system was gradually crumbling under my own analysis.

I racked my brain and could think of no conversation or Wiccan text that told me how to cope with this situation.

I thought believing hard enough in the goddess made her real. Well then, where is she? Goddess, I need you in my life now more than ever, where are you?

I was met with a silence so cold it chilled me to the bone.

Disgust, bitterness, and weary determination drove my thoughts.

But church? How can I go there? They'll hate me. I quickly recalled all the evils done to pagans in the name of Christianity. Those who have been spit on, lost their jobs, lost custody of their children, been heckled as Satan worshipers, and had their cars and homes vandalized, and the piles of Neo-pagan books self-righteous Christians had burned on television. Years before, an elderly Christian woman firmly grabbed me by the forearm while waving tracts in my face and telling me my child would burn in hell. I never understood what makes Christians think if they treat someone like garbage, that person will then turn around and say, "Hey, I want to be just like you! Sign me up for Christianity!" Cruelty never brings people to Christ. Why is that so hard for Christians to understand?

But the thought of going to a church filled me with a crippling fear. Do I know enough to go to church? Only Christians attend church. I don't belong there.

I felt so frightened and alone in my grief. I desperately needed a faith to cling to. After weeks of arguing with myself, I decided I needed to talk to one of them, a Christian.

But who? I know so few. What Christian could I trust enough to open up to with my tumult of questions?

I realized there was only one I knew of: the Christian I had labeled "It." I rationalized I would be safe if I kept my mouth shut. I'll talk to It but no one else.

### "I Need to Be Saved"

I walked through the front doors and announced my presence to the secretary who graciously waved me inside. I'd never been in a pastor's office before. Until the previous day, I hadn't even known such things existed. I assumed pastors preached on Sunday and then went home. The pastor sat in a leather chair directly across from me. I had expected him to remain seated at his desk farther away—separate.

This feels somewhat intimate, I thought uneasily.

I opened the conversation by expressing my gratitude at his having come to my home the night Randy was killed. We spoke briefly of the accident and then I told him why I had really come.

"I need to be saved," I said.

His look of shock would have amused me if I hadn't already been so full of apprehension.

He seemed thrilled at bringing another sheep into the flock and eagerly dove into the message of Christ's salvation and how I too could have it.

I was still fearful though—and distracted. I needed to swallow. I took another drink of water.

He was talking too fast regarding things I knew nothing about; he nearly lost me in the conversation.

I have to stop this. He needs to know the whole truth before we go on.

I nervously interrupted him. "There is more you need to know concerning my past." I feared my past was so tainted that I would be unacceptable to the Christian God or his followers. I fully expected judgment and accusations, and to be thrown out with an angry declaration I was never to pass through these church doors again.

As I spoke, I slowly slipped my hand into my jacket pocket and formed a fist around its contents, my pentagram necklace. This was the one thing that represented my former faith more than any other item I owned. It had been a most cherished possession, and it was the first piece of pagan jewelry I had carefully chosen and purchased. I wore it as a symbol of protection and always had it on during spell work. I had loved it and worn this necklace with pride for many years. I felt it could be an offering, symbolic of a passing from the sham of a faith I had held onto for so long, into the reality and hope of Christianity.

"I trust you more that you will ever know," I said out loud to him. As I spoke, I handed him the pentagram.

"What's this?" Durwin asked. He reached for it without hesitation. It shocked me; I had expected it to repulse him.

"My pentagram," I said. "The reason I'm not saved is that I'm Wiccan. I have been a solitary practitioner..." I paused "...of witchcraft." I waited for the axe to fall, but he simply looked at me curiously. Did he not comprehend? Where's the fire and brimstone? When are they going to burn me at the stake?

"Really?" he asked. "Tell me more about it." He inspected the pentagram. "What does this mean?"

I did a mental double take. What is he up to? Is this some

sort of game? How can he not know anything about witchcraft? Didn't all Christian's have an instant hatred of anything pagan?

It confused me. He seemed genuinely interested without the slightest bit of animosity evident on his face. I looked at him doubtfully and then forged ahead, describing Wicca to him in the most sanitized version I could. "We worship nature, not Satan. The greater holidays correspond with the vernal equinoxes, solstices, and seasons. The lesser holidays correspond with the full and new moons."

He listened intently.

He seemed fascinated; his receptiveness caught me completely off guard.

"The pentagram is a symbol of protection, not evil," I explained. "There are covens, but I never joined one, I worked alone."

I spoke of Wicca for some time. He eventually stopped me and reminded me of my visit's original intentions: my desire to be a Christian. It occurred to me later that he never asked me why I wanted to be saved. The only thing that seemed important to him was that I desired it with all my heart. He said it only required my saying a simple prayer that spoke of my desire for Jesus to be my Lord and Savior and to forgive me of my sins. He said I could repeat a prayer he spoke or I could say a prayer myself.

I said, "It's been a long time since I have said a prayer, Durwin."

He looked at the pentagram now lying on the side table, poked it with his finger, and said, "I bet it has."

So with bowed heads, I repeated a simple prayer after him that committed my life to Jesus. When we had finished, I remember him looking at me, smiling, and saying, "Amen." He was very pleased.

I didn't feel like smiling though. I felt tearful. I had expected a more pronounced change in myself. I knew and believed that I was saved—I did not doubt that. But I was still fearful, and I realized this was only the beginning of my journey; I still had much work to do involving my walk in Christianity. I was born again, and very much a newborn. Besides, They were still outside, waiting for me.

It was soon time for me to go. As we both stood, he gave me a hug welcoming me into the flock. I realized it would take many months if not years of spiritual growth for me to express to him what becoming a Christian had meant to me. But I had time.

I exited the church doors with the feeling of an almost imperceptible weight having been lifted from me. I crossed the parking lot and looked up, thinking, Is the sky bluer than when I went in? Maybe.

*Read more of Shari (Hadley) Pruitt's gripping testimony in her enlightening book,* **From The Cauldron to the Cross***, available in e-book format at most major E-book retailers.*

# FROM THE CRAFT TO CHRIST

# CHAPTER NINETEEN

―᙮―

## Bridget Birkner

*Bridget grew up dancing to the beat of a different drum in her local cathedral. Desiring a deeper spirituality that wasn't found within its stone-cold walls left her vulnerable to the Enemy's lies. Her journey led her down the Christopaganism path toward her chosen destiny as a Christian witch until the real Jesus confronted her in the most surreal way.*

I was Lady Aine Willowfae, the leader of The Circle of the Sacred Woodland, a multi-faith group of approximately sixty people from the Delaware Valley (Pennsylvania, New Jersey, and Delaware). It's spring as I write my testimony and reflect on this time three years ago. I was gearing up for the biggest celebration of the year. In just a few short days, we would erect a maypole for our Bealtaine festival. (Bealtaine is the beginning of summer and is a fertility festival. The maypole is a large pole, used as a phallic symbol, with ribbons that men and women use in a ribbon dance in part of the fertility rite). We would soon dance around the maypole with ribbons and flowers, praising the goddess for the bounty of spring.

It was a magickal time when I believed fairies and gnomes, angels and water sprites would come out and make merry with us. I was an ordained high priestess of my order, which resulted in The Circle of the Sacred Woodland's formation. I led full- and new-moon rituals and led the circle in Sabbat celebrations. Though I mainly stayed within pagan traditions, I always felt the need to allow all faiths to be a part of the circle because my path

~ 237

was not a religion, but more of a philosophy. The witchcraft I practiced focused on Celtic and Native American shamanism and included certain parts of Christianity to create a path that not only felt beautiful to walk on, but also felt right. After three years, I abruptly closed The Circle of the Sacred Woodland, and until this day, people still question the reason of its demise.

What many did not realize at the time was that I had a supernatural encounter that changed my life. In fact, it virtually rewired my brain. Talk about the power of God! And here I am three years later, typing out my testimony and how thankful I am to my heavenly Father for pulling me out of the occult. It was one of the hardest yet most liberating experiences of my life.

## Raised on Catholicism

I was born and raised in Chester County, Pennsylvania, in a strict Roman Catholic household. I attended Catholic school from elementary on up through high school and was an integral part of the church community. During my years growing up as a Catholic, I never read the Bible. The priest taught that the Bible was not the literal Word of God, but more of a symbol used to live like Christ; that the Old Testament was allegorical; and that the New Testament was just observations from the disciples.

It was clear to my family and friends I was different, as I was always a lone wolf dancing to the beat of my own drum. Embracing this difference, I ran with it, to the point I felt God created me to "break the mold" from societal norms. I craved being off the beaten path, and I do not believe there is anything wrong with that. My desire to become part of the Craft was born from that, as well as my need to feel connected to something spiritual. I understand now this radical nonconformist nature within me could have been used for the kingdom, but instead the Enemy took it for his bidding.

After getting married and having my first child, I felt a shift in my spiritual beliefs and began to focus on things outside of Roman Catholicism. I had an affinity toward magick and other alternative forms of therapy, such as Reiki. I became interested in angels and used angel cards as my primary form of divination. I received messages that I believed were from my guardian angels and spiritual guides, saints, and even Jesus Himself. I believed that I was a vessel for all energetic beings, ascending to a higher level of enlightenment so I could be a beacon to those looking for God. Feeling powerful boosted my ego and self-worth, and even though I know I tried to remain humble, I felt pride rising within me.

## A Christian Witches Brew

Once my marriage ended, I put all my energies into my son and my new magickal path. At that point, I dove heavily into learning about different cultures around the world and alternative spirituality, and found my home in Celtic and Native American shamanism. I practiced witchcraft I considered to be white magick. Dark magick was off limits as I still believed in God and the Trinity, and held a devotion to Jesus and Mary.

As a Solitary Witch, I felt the need to "dress the part." From clothing to jewelry, makeup to hairstyles, I wanted to be a gypsy bohemian—a sexual and powerful female at one with the Earth. Paganism was darker than what I was used to, and yet it fascinated me to my core. I loved it not just for the rituals, clothing, and music, but because I felt I could hold myself accountable for the choices in my life, rather than feel like I needed permission from some heavenly parental figure up in the skies. For a while, I laid low and continued to practice as a Catholic while secretly delving deeper into paganism. Ironically, I still loved Jesus and believed in my heart that my love for Him grew from my studies. I now identified as a Christian pagan or witch.

I sold my services of tarot, oracle, and spiritual consultation on my blog and website. Looking back now, I had so many opportunities to follow God's path, knowing full well the Bible said these things were abominations. But I used my Catholic upbringing to excuse myself for my behavior because it was all allegorical, right? I figured that as long as I felt I was doing good and wasn't hurting anyone, then God must be happy with me.

After several years I started moving toward a darker path and dedicated myself to the goddess Hecate, known as the goddess of witches. After reading a book by Sorita d'Este, I incorporated the rite of Hecate's sacred fires into my own ritual. In my ritual garb, I'd smudge the area with sage, call the four quarters (North, East, South, and West) as the wind kicked up, and sealed the circle with my athame (ritual knife) to create sacred space. Standing before my altar, I'd ask Jesus, Mary, and all the angels and saints to protect me as I began lighting the candles and incense. I called upon the goddess Hecate and asked her to provide details into my life, and felt her presence enter my circle. Then I'd meditate, looking deeply into the flames of the candle that flickered erratically, and listen for her voice. If I saw anything, I'd write it down and go to a book I used for insight in interpreting what I had seen.

## Handmaiden for Mother Earth

I left the Catholic Church and became open about loving my Earth Spirituality, which I called it because paganism has a societal stigma that causes people to believe that all who practice it are devil-worshiping, animal-sacrificing followers of Satan. I conducted my studies through Sagefyre, a female-inclusive group, then became a leader in the community, guiding and teaching like-minded individuals who saw and felt the same as I did. I thought I was home in my newfound faith—being able to love God, Jesus, Mary, and the angels and saints, all while dedicating myself to Mother Earth by committing myself to the fundamentals of holding rituals honoring not just them, but all the deities that all the cultures in the world comprised. I felt I was coexisting with Mother Earth herself and I was a handmaiden to her services. As the years passed, I realized Jesus, Mary, the saints, and the angels started to take a back burner to other deities whom I wanted to learn about and study.

In autumn of 2016, I studied Hinduism and was listening to a lot of Hindi music, while trying to practice some festival rituals held on the other side of the world. Two weeks later, I fell off the proverbial ledge and went underground (like Persephone in the old Greek tales). I lingered down there, because my desire to dig deeper while not being 100 percent comfortable with my pagan identity troubled my soul. I felt a weight on my shoulders, and my chest was so heavy that I couldn't breathe—or explain it. A deep depression set in, and then it happened.

## The Living Water

On the evening of November 18, 2016, I had the house to myself and retreated to a hot relaxing shower. I had just finished washing my hair in the steamy shower when I turned my head to the side and saw Him. Jesus was formed within the shower wall. He was beautiful to behold: big brown eyes, wavy long hair, a beard, and olive-colored skin. It stunned me and I started to freak out, even slapping my face, saying, "This can't be happening! This must be a dream! This can't be real!"

His expression became sad, and He posed a question to me: "Daughter, when did I become not enough for you?" I just stood there speechless. He asked it again, and with my lack of response, He said, "There's a song you used to sing. I like to think of it as our song. Will you sing it for Me?"

A song suddenly came to my memory. It was one I sang as a little girl in the Catholic Church. The name of the song was "Hosea," and as the words fell from my lips.... they now took on a whole new meaning. It was an intimate love song calling me, the estranged one home. It touched on how I strayed into the wilderness, yet reassured me that He had been there all along, patiently awaiting my return. It was His song for me and the words spoke to my heart with tenderness and desire for us to live deeply in our new life together.

What I didn't realize until after I stopped singing was that I was in such a state of sadness, my eyes felt like they were swelling shut. I don't know how long I was crying. Then I heard, "Come back to Me, Bridget. Come back to Me, my sweet daughter. Come back to Me."

I looked up and saw Him looking at me with such sadness and disappointment. I denied what I saw, shaking my head and crying out, "You're not here! You're not here! I'm dreaming, or delusional!" I turned away.

Next thing I remember, I felt this overwhelming dread. He said, "If you truly want to know how it feels to not have Me here, you will experience my absence." And then it seemed everything stopped. I no longer saw Him or heard anything but the shower running, and I remember looking around and realizing He was gone. Immediately I experienced a pain in my heart and a darkness so deep that I couldn't breathe. Everything around me was like a living hell, and I was drowning in it. This was distinctly disturbing because I knew this presence wasn't of God. It was as if I'd lost every loved one and I wanted to disappear. I never felt so alone in my life as I did at that moment. I started to panic and scream, but realized no one would hear me. Shame washed right through me as I fell into despair. I screamed out to God, "No! Don't do it! Don't leave me! Noooo!" I clawed the shower walls as if trying to escape the torment, but no one was there to save me. Then everything went dark.

Next thing I recall, I was kneeling in the shower with the water still running, but it was cold as ice. I felt vulnerable and numb as I knelt there, almost prostrate, begging Jesus to come back. I was so shamed and hopeless, like this was it and God had left me. And it was all my fault, and I would have to live with this for the rest of my life and never feel Him again. As I continued sobbing, this electricity flowed through me and I heard a faint shushing sound, hushing me to stop my tears. Within seconds, I felt a warm embrace around my body. My chest tightened, and I realized it was Him. He was back, and He said, "Welcome back, daughter. I missed you."

I started to cry again, but He kept hushing me, reassuring me it was all right and that He needed me to feel a modicum of the life those in hell were living without His presence. I don't know how long I was lying in there, but it was long enough. Too long, perhaps. He told me that when I woke up the next day, I would be on a new path—a path of joy and a path of tears. I would lose many people in my life because of this, but I would gain a new community that was stronger in faith for Him. And that He was leading me now toward my steps in ministry. That my days as a free-loving pagan were over. I would make sacrifices and chapters of my life would close, but it would all bring me to Him.

## My Resurrection

Over an hour later, I walked out of the bathroom a different person. From that night, the Holy Spirit convicted me to read the Bible and go to church because I needed to feel close to God again. I went back to the Unitarian Church I attended in the past, where I had a few friends, and continued to go there for weeks, until I realized I wanted to become a member. This church was open to all faiths, but one thing required was that church members were not to believe in the Trinity. I've always been a believer in the triune God, so I concluded that I didn't belong there and didn't go back.

At the request of a couple friends, I went to a Christian church just a couple blocks from my home. The church welcomed me in with open arms and opened my spiritual eyes with divine teaching. Five months later, I was baptized as a born-again Christian. At the moment Pastor Wayne submerged me under the water, I thought, This is my funeral, Satan. You can't bother me anymore because I am dead. I knew at the moment I rose out of that water as a new child of God that everything I had done was forgiven. Along with the birth of my son, this event was the most amazing moment in my life.

Since my baptism in 2017, I have read the Bible cover to cover, joined the worship team, and become active with Philia Ministries. I'm also a recent graduate of Elijah House Prayer Ministry. Sadly, a pagan friend I considered like a sister attacked me on social media for coming back to Jesus. This woman—who I confided in, loved so much, and had given an open-door invitation to our home—turned so cruel that it's something I still think about years later. I'm no stranger to controversy in my transition from paganism to Christ, and most of my pagan friends have been kind and honest with me, even if it hurts them that I no longer believe in the things I once did.

Although I encounter spiritual warfare daily, I wake up every morning with such joy in my heart for being given this chance to witness to this world, and I go to bed every night knowing that even if I screwed up during the day, God's unconditional love and my faith in Him is what carries me through the night and into the next day. Jesus is my everlasting, and my life is completely devoted to Him. Looking back over my life, it is ironic to think I was researching and studying all beliefs except for the one my parents had brought me up in. It took a miracle to find the truth that I had taken for granted and thought I already knew.

I am now Bridget Birkner, a daughter of the King, a bride of Christ Jesus, and the apple of His eye.

Yes, Jesus, you are more than enough.

## CHAPTER TWENTY

## Evidence of Prayer

After reading the testimonies of these former witches, I realized a common thread evident in most of their stories. Almost every one had at least one if not more believers praying for them during their involvement in witchcraft. The former witch may not have even known someone was praying, but that commitment to pray brought what had seemed impossible, to happen in God's perfect timing. Suddenly the veil that had clouded their eyes and thwarted their understanding of God's truth was removed and the light of Jesus overcame the darkness they had not known existed.

Prayer is powerful, and few realize the strength God has given us in having the ability to engage in it. Our prayer should be our passion, and if our hearts are motivated by the same love of our heavenly Father, we cannot help but long to see the prodigals come home. This passion should further motivate us to pray earnestly for those denying God's Word and His will in their lives, and for those who worship other gods. It should stir us to pray until the whole earth has seen His goodness.

> *Our prayer should be our passion, and if our hearts are motivated by the same love of our heavenly Father, we cannot help but long to see the prodigals come home.*

## Prayer from a Long-Lost Friend—Mike

When Mike was in college, his closest friend, Al, was a Christian. Over time they gradually lost touch with one another. After having been out of touch for over a decade, they caught up with one another and rekindled their friendship. Al shared how, ten years prior, his pastor had told all the men of the church to choose just one person and to pray for them every day. Al felt led to commit to pray for Mike, and for ten years, practically every day, he brought Mike before the Lord in prayer.

Al had no way of knowing what Mike had become involved in; he was just being faithful, and Mike knows today that Al's faithful prayers over those long years were responsible for his being able to escape the entanglements of witchcraft and the occult.

> *God is still in the miracle business and He is still mighty to save.*
> —Mike Morton

Mike shares his heart on praying for those involved in occult activity: "Please know in your heart that the greatest thing you can do is pray for them. God is still in the miracle business and He is still mighty to save. That person needs your fervent, faithful, ongoing prayer to break the bonds and chains that bind them. Never forget that Satan has been defeated at the cross and at the empty tomb. It may require weeks, months, or even years of prayer, and may require you to fast, but Christ in you makes you a mighty warrior. If the Lord burdens you to intercede for someone engaged in the occult, then follow through faithfully, knowing that the gates of hell will not prevail, and who God sets free is free indeed (John 8:34–36)."

## Praying with a Heart of Compassion—Lupe

Lupe's coworker, who later became her husband, was the praying warrior God used to intercede on her behalf. Her involvement in witchcraft was obvious because of the pentacle she wore. Peter approached with a nonjudgmental attitude and a lot of prayer, even gathering prayer support from outside churches. He shared books, life experiences, and friendship as a way of reaching beyond her strong spirit and the demonic forces at work.

Peter's advice for those wanting to help those involved in witchcraft is, "You must pray, pray, gently lead, be patient, persevere, love the truth, and know the Bible."

### The Changing of the Guard—Selah Ally

For a while, I was a regular on the church elders' meeting agenda, as my pastors and their wives, along with other church members aware of my involvement, set time aside during each meeting to pray for me. These men and women of God faithfully prayed for years despite not seeing any fruit for their efforts, and they questioned if they should continue or if my mocking attitude was evidence of the Enemy's plot to distract them from God's plan.

Pastor Lyndon shared about one evening when he spent a significant amount of time praying as I was tempted and went to a ritual during my coming-out stage. I later conveyed how I had walked into chaos and disarray with little magick accomplished that night, confirming the effect and impact his prayers had on our physical reality.

After years of pressing in, these prayer warriors were growing weary when God sent a second wind of intercession. Bo, being new to my situation, came with a refreshing zeal. He called upon two churches, one in Arizona and another in California, to hold me in prayer and intercession during their weekly prayer meetings, firmly believing in the Scripture that "when two or three are gathered in My name, I am there in the midst of them" (Matthew 18:20). Bo shared, "Many times in our emails or phone conversations, I witnessed opportunities ... small breakthroughs like a change in her tone of voice or a willingness to discuss the Word of God

*My life is evidence of the power of prayer.*

when the doors of her heart were previously locked."

I can attest that many times my outward physical actions were more a manifestation of the spiritual war within, and not a true reflection of my heart. I thank God for those who relentlessly brought me before His throne and that they were not deterred by time or my reaction, but rather pushed forward until a breakthrough took place. God heard His servants' cries and answered their prayers to soften my heart and supernaturally reveal Himself. My life is evidence of the power of prayer.

### Six Hours to Salvation—Victoria

It all began in an online discussion group whose style of communication was an exchange of hostile fire by both Christians and nonbelievers. God made it clear to Charles that his approach should showcase being on the offensive without being offensive and to answer questions in a way that would glorify Christ. Victoria posed a thought-provoking question to Charles, and his prayer journey began. He began witnessing to her, and once he combined the element of prayer, he experienced spiritual pressures he had never encountered before.

When hell became the conversation topic, the spiritual attacks intensified. Charles's six-year-old son had terrifying nightmares and his home was under spiritual attack, but Charles pressed in with a righteous anger and did not relent, continuing to pray for Victoria's salvation. He soon faced an entity that attempted to distract, discourage, and instill fear, but he spoke directly to it, saying, "At the end of the day I will go to heaven, but you have no such redemption," and with that, the power broke.

An important lesson he learned is that it is not about winning an argument but sharing on an emotional level about your feelings and heart toward God. Feeling in his spirit that he needed to pray one day, Charles spent at least six hours in prayer until he received a call from Victoria, and she received salvation that very day.

## A Father's Love—Taryn

Taryn shared that her father and his entire congregation of ten prayed for her. She believes their prayers protected her and were eventually what led her to the Lord. Taryn testifies, "The power of prayer is like nothing I've ever seen before!"

## The Persistence of a Praying Grandmother—Ron

Ron shared that when he was growing up, his grandmother had always said she was praying for him and that God would make him a preacher. At thirteen, during one of the last times he was in church, someone prophesied that he would be an evangelist in his thirties.

Ron remembered none of this until after he was saved, and upon going through his old storage, he found a Nave's Topical Bible set that his grandmother had given him for Christmas when he was twelve. He used it for the first few years of his outreach ministry, and explains how he was still a heathen and a full-blown witch when she passed away. She had not lived to see prophesy fulfilled, but he believes her years of prayers had more to do with it than anything else.

## The Fervent Prayer of a Mother—Shalom

Both Shalom's mother and grandmother prayed for her throughout her involvement in the Craft. She knows their prayers kept her from harm, even death, and from becoming more deeply dedicated. Shalom explains, "I took many risks that resulted in less harm than had been probable, and attempted many rituals to conjure that were not nearly as successful as they could have been."

After Shalom was born again, she found out that her mother had recently changed her prayers to be not only for her safety but also for her salvation, and was certain that made a significant difference. Shalom is convinced that it is very important and effective to pray for those who are following the Craft, and to pray especially for their salvation!

Her mother shared how she thanks Yahweh every day that He brought Shalom to the truth. Today, they pray together each evening and read the Word each night. During the day, her mother still prays for Yahweh to help her and so often she sees Him working in Shalom's life.

## Unknowing Recipient—Mark

While Mark does not know of anyone who prayed for him during his involvement in witchcraft, his lovely wife shared how her father had been praying for his daughter's future husband since her birth. So in a roundabout way, Mark was the recipient of prayer even though he never knew about it.

## Prayer of the Saints—April

Several people were praying for April, including her mother who was a practicing Catholic. Her aunt and uncle, also Catholic, prayed and encouraged her to talk with their priest when she was struggling. A friend whom she had worked with at the psychic hotline and had converted to Christianity, told her she also was praying, and several other Christians prayed over the years and many reached out and tried to share the gospel.

April always accepted offers of prayer, believing it would be "positive energy" or bring good into her life by the "law of attraction." At the time, she did not understand about having a relationship with Jesus. She shares, "I am certain that many of the prayers by followers of Christ were heard by Him, and that God was working in my life long before I realized He was."

## Divine Intervention—Carrie

Who would have thought that working at a woman's shelter you would find a pastor and a witch sitting side by side? Carrie became frustrated with the pastor's never-ending smile and the constant reminder that "Jesus loves you" despite her confession of being a witch and a high priestess. What she had not realized at the time was the pastor was praying for her and had received direct instruction from God on her behalf. The Lord had told him not to let her harsh words affect him, as Satan had put those thoughts in her mind. Rather, he was to lean not on his own understanding but only on God's wisdom. God promised to chip away the wall of hate and rebellion.

It is hard not to take offense when someone is spewing insults at God and you, but that did not stop this pastor's perseverance. He prayed against the rebellious spirit, for the Holy Spirit to convict her heart, and that she would become displeased with witchcraft. At night, Carrie would hear his words, "Jesus loves you," until she finally accepted his invitation to church. Once there, her eyes were opened and she was set free.

Carrie's pastor shares this encouragement: "Only Jesus can work on the heart of one who is lost ... and He loves every one of them no matter what. He left the ninety-nine to find Carrie, and He will do the same for you!"

### Warfare Prayer 911 - Shari

Durwin, the police chaplain who came to Shari's aid after her husband's tragic car accident, knew how to pray for her grief and pain but not for the spiritual battle that lie ahead. He heard of her Wicca involvement at the same time he led her in a salvation prayer. Soon after, he would learn how to pray against demonic oppression, as Shari heard voices and experienced demonic manifestations even after becoming a Christ-follower.

Durwin shares, "These kinds of experiences were new to me, so I prayed for God to give Shari, as well as me, wisdom in dealing with these evil forces. God answered that prayer by connecting Shari with a lady involved in Freedom in Christ Ministries (FIC).[11] Through FIC, God delivered Shari from the lies, deception, and empty threats of our enemy. I'll never forget the day Shari walked in to church after praying through the Steps to Freedom, and asking, 'Is it always this quiet?' She no longer had demonic voices wreaking havoc in her ears and mind!"

---

[11] See Neil T. Anderson, *The Steps to Freedom in Christ* (Bloomington, Minnesota: Bethany House, 2001).

## In His Timing - Bridget

Steven first met Bridget at a party at the home of his girlfriend, who had filled him in on her pagan spirituality. It was obvious to Steven that Bridget was seeking to fill a spiritual void, and he began to pray for two things: that God would make Himself unquestionably real to her and that if the Lord wanted to use him, that He would do so in His own timing.

As a result of his prayers, Bridget and Steven had an open dialogue that contained many friendly conversations about faith. God proved to be faithful as Bridget experienced Him in the most tangible way possible. Furthermore, the Lord saw fit to stitch their lives closer in not only friendship, but as co-heirs with Christ.

Steven proclaimed, "Praise God that He works His will in His time and with whomever He desires."

## Conclusion

What should the church's response be when confronted with the involvement of witchcraft? We cannot fail to recognize the areas where we, the church, have allowed man-made idolatries to take residence within our walls, nor can we underestimate the extent to which the worm has slithered into our theology. It is time we get our focus back on God and resist the temptation to experiment with universal philosophies that will surely lead us to question away our salvation.

Rather than disregard the move of the Holy Spirit or subject ourselves to spiritual counterfeits, we need to use the gift of discernment and allow His Spirit to guide us under His living Word. Above all, we need to reveal the love of God in our lives and in our love for one another so that the entire world can see His love, through us.

> *If we are really going to reach them, we need to have the same crazy passionate heart for them that God has for us.*

You have now read the stories of

those who once rejected the cross in lieu of the Craft, and witnessed the amazing act of Jesus' redemption that brought each one back into the loving arms of Almighty God. In their lives you have seen the well-intended efforts of the church become a stumbling block, but fortunately, you have also witnessed those who have heeded the leading of the Holy Spirit to become participants of God's mighty work.

Ironically, Christians have gone from being cold and callused to the witch, to the point of incorporating witchcraft practices in our sanctuary. Neither extreme leads to Jesus. If we are really going to reach them, we need to have the same crazy passionate heart for them that God has for us—right where they are.

Isn't that where God met you?

# FROM THE CRAFT TO CHRIST

"Though I speak with the tongues of men and of angels, but have not love, I have become sounding brass or a clanging cymbal. And though I have *the gift of* prophecy, and understand all mysteries and all knowledge, and though I have all faith, so that I could remove mountains, but have not love, I am nothing. And though I bestow all my goods to feed *the poor*, and though I give my body to be burned, but have not love, it profits me nothing."

1 Corinthians 13:1-3

# APPENDIX

# A Letter to a Wiccan

Charles wrote this prophetic letter to Victoria during her struggle between Wicca and Jehovah. These God-inspired words will make a dramatic impact on you, as they did on Victoria, revealing one of the internal battles that may also take place in your own spiritual life.

Dear Friend,

I see your heart fighting against your will. "I have felt God," says your heart. "And I want Him. I want to experience that love again." The will responds, "No, I won't lay aside what I found in Wicca." While the will suppresses the heart, it cannot eradicate the longing. I certainly encourage you to speak and write to Christians about this Jehovah that you do not know, but in the end it will come down to the fight between ... your will and ... your heart. Your heart will continue longing for Jehovah and your will continues to resist.

You have two options: shut God out or let God in. Wicca will get you so far to God but no further since you are doing the active part. You now have a situation where God is doing the active part, inviting you into that close communion with Him. If Wicca could provide what God really offers ... intimate union with the divine, you would not have this longing. It cannot. Only accepting the invitation for the indwelling of God can fill that void. I'm trying to tell you what I found, and I can see how strongly your heart is seeking it. From my heart to yours ... let Him in.

"**A Witch's Encounter with God -Taken from the Night**" engages the reader immediately and transports them to the battlefield of the soul. This compelling narrative pulls no punches about church life, family struggles, and the darkness that often parades as light!"
~ Dr. Ron Phillips, Senior Pastor of Abba's House and author of over 30 books, including *Our Invisible Allies*

Ms. Tower's first-hand account exposes a thread the enemy uses to entice and ensnare his captive and reveals the unraveling beauty of grace.

Available in paperback and e-book format at your favorite book retailer.

"He had a very menacing evil grin, as though he were relishing every moment of my suffering . . . I knew he was a dangerous combination of intelligence and ingenuity and he would be angry at my conversion to Christianity."
~Shari (Hadley) Pruitt

**"From the Cauldron to the Cross"**

Follow Shari on her path to freedom and learn how you, too, can be free from sin's damaging control.

Available at your favorite e-book retailer.

www.ingramcontent.com/pod-product-compliance
Lightning Source LLC
Chambersburg PA
CBHW050629300426
44112CB00012B/1718